BIPOLAR DEPRESSI

From Both Sides Of The Couch

A Memoir / Self-Help Guide To Wellness

By

Pamela G. Cohen, M.A.

First Edition

Note: The information in this book is intended only for an informative guide for those wishing to know more about mental health issues. In no way is this book intended to replace, countermand or conflict with the advice of your physician or caregiver. The ultimate decisions should be made in consultation between you and your professional handling your case.

Catalog-in-Publication Data. Cohen, Pamela G. Bipolar Depression and Me: From Both Sides of the Couch. Includes Bibliography and Sources for Further Information.

1   Mental Illness
2   Bipolar Disorder
3   Depression
4   Hypersexual Behavior
5   Psychology Training
6   PLAN Clubhouse of Dallas County, Texas

Dewy Decimal Number: 616.89

ISBN 9798387206245

Cover Designed by Jean Picazo

Dedication

This book is dedicated to my family who always loved me even in my most difficult times, and for all the people I know and have not yet met who suffer in silence with mental illness.

PLEASE, NEVER GIVE UP THE FIGHT TO LIVE!

TABLE OF CONTENTS

PART I: THE OTHER SIDE OF THE COUCH   **6**

Chapter One: Innocence Collides with the Beast   7

Chapter Two: The BEAST is Identified   32

Chapter Three: The Beast Confronts the Therapist   39

Chapter Four: The BEAST and Relationships; Me, Him and my Illness   46

Chapter Five: Moving, Mania and Mixed Episodes   65

Chapter Six: The Beginning and Waning of Hope   73

Chapter Seven: Hope Becomes Reality   82

PART II: THE OTHER SIDE OF THE COUCH   **91**

Chapter Eight: Understanding the BEAST from My Perspective   92

Chapter Nine: Understanding the Effects of the Illness   106

Chapter Ten: The Side Effects of Medicine, Illness and Knowing the Difference   130

Chapter Eleven: Recovery   134

Conclusion   149

Bibliography   151

Websites   154

Periodicals   155

Acknowledgments   156

About the Author   157

PART I: MY SIDE OF THE COUCH

In Part I of this book, I share my experiences of living with Bipolar Disorder for over four decades. I share my struggles and successes as I fought for my stability with this incurable but manageable mental illness. Hopefully, by reading my memoir you will be able to escape some pitfalls and find hope and courage in my story. It is my wish that people suffering from these illnesses and their family members use this book as a guide to enhance recovery.

Chapter One: Innocence Collides with the BEAST

I was 19 years old when bipolar disorder aka the "BEAST" made an entry in my life. However, it did not erupt in a single day like a volcano, but came along slowly with various warning signs. Meanwhile, a long time had passed by before I was diagnosed correctly, before I could make any sense of what was happening to me. It was all so very scary. I felt as if my brain had broken, as if a tornado had run through my mind and left me with a pile of wreckage to stand on. I could not seem to get my brain back on firmer ground. It took as long as fifteen years to be correctly diagnosed, and longer to get the correct medicine regime for my disease.

The year was 1978. I was first diagnosed with unipolar depression, what they now call MDD (Major Depressive Disorder). I had manic episodes off and on that went largely unnoticed for quite some time. Come to think of it, this lack of awareness regarding my bipolar disorder was not unusual, especially during those days. According to various sources and case studies I later delved into, I got to know that it now takes an average of eight years to be diagnosed correctly with bipolar disorder, owing to the complexity of the disease, the fact that most people seek help only when they are depressed, and that self-reports to psychiatrists are not all that great. In addition, other diseases can mimic bipolar disorder such as hypothyroidism, PTSD, and drug abuse, to name a few. One can go to NAMI.org (National Alliance of Mental Illness) or other organizations listed in the website and bibliography sections of this book, and search for bipolar disorder to learn more. There are two commonly known types of bipolar disorder, bipolar 1 which means you have at least one episode of mania and depressive episodes, and bipolar 11 in which one has hypomania (less severe form of mania) along with depressive episodes. (Understanding Mental Disorders: Your Guide to DSM-5 Washington, DC: American Psychiatric Association, 2015)

I will be sharing my experiences with bipolar 1, but my tryst with depression has been far more excruciating than it has been with mania. The first part of this book as I mentioned earlier, is a memoir which is my personal journey with bipolar disorder. The second part of this book, on the other hand, consists of valuable information that I have gained through my many years of personal experience with the disorder. Apart from my own personal experiences, I also observed others struggling with bipolar disorder through my eight years of professional experience as a Director of

Education/Socialization working with people who struggled with severe and persistent mental illnesses(SMI) including bipolar disorder, MDD, schizoaffective disorder, and schizophrenia. Additionally, I have gained experience as a graduate student in clinical psychology in which I earned a Master's Degree, in 1998. My observations regarding the disease are documented from those experiences. However, having said that, I must add that this book is not a substitute for getting help from a psychiatrist or a trained therapist.

At the very outset of this journey, I would like to share some information about the formative years of my life. Apparently, I had a normal upbringing with normal mood swings, like any other child my age. I grew up in a middle-class neighborhood in Portland, Maine, which happened to be the most populated city in state. In the 1970's, the state had approximately 69,000 people, and the population was multiplying every year. It was a tough place to live; with the long, blizzard-filled winters months, when your best friend was your shovel. The people looked older than their age, they were pale-skinned with wrinkles on their faces from the long winter months and freezing temperatures, with little exposure to sunlight. It got dark at 4 pm. The summers were short, usually July till August. I was actually born in a place and time where "rugged individualism" was the norm, meaning that people around me were self-reliant. Mainers are tough, resilient individuals, and possess a strong down east accent that excludes the letter "R". The locals were, and are, to date, very stoic, and self-sufficient. Mainers believe in quick problem solving and action. They don't have a lot of time at their disposal for down time or for emotional processing. One has to just put his nose to the grindstone and keep going. This spirit of rugged individualism which was somehow ingrained in me unknowingly, helped me keep going when my illness got tough. Therefore, I was a very functional individual, even when I was in the severe pain of depression. I just wouldn't be knocked down, until I was. Fortitude is a gift that can be learned if one reaches within himself to seek it, and I did just the same, i.e., reached within myself.

In 1978, when my illness was diagnosed, stamps cost thirteen cents apiece, and the price of gasoline was sixty-three cents a gallon, which is inconceivable in today's times. The movie "Grease" was Number One at the box office. Small Pox was eradicated, and the first in-vitro human child was born. The blizzard of 1978 that hit New England and New York stopped almost everything as towns were snowed in. During that turbulent period, my mind was gradually being transformed to the blizzard outside of me, unnerving and relentless, leaving me paralyzed, mentally and emotionally. On the other hand, when my disease occurred, psychoanalysis was popular in the mainstream American culture. The idea was to make the unconscious conscious, to give context and meaning to our behavior, our outbursts. In 1978, the psychoanalysts had patients lying on the couch while they sat behind them and said, "Aha," like Freud. The patients were encouraged to speak uninhibitedly, without editing their thoughts. The therapists were more eclectic, full of insight and understanding, using techniques from many famous theorists in their practices. And, the patient sat on the couch across from the therapist while conversing. The therapists, explained depression as a form of anger turned inward, and mania as a flight or an escape from depression. For the psychiatrists, lithium was the answer. It might have been helpful to some others, however, most of the therapists' techniques were not helpful to my own unique plight, for it was biological, and lithium did not work for me.

In the 60's and 70's, I grew up on a street with many kids my age, mostly boys. Therefore, as a tom-boy, I spent a lot of time playing basketball, football, and baseball. Up to a point in my childhood, I was the best at all of these sports, until adolescence came around and the boys grew like weeds, and I started menstruating. It was a bummer. My middle sister, Bonnie, taunted me the night before I started menstruating. She remarked in jest that I was going to get my period due to my moodiness in the days leading up to it. Little did she know how this prediction was actually a foreshadowing of countless mood swings that followed, wreaking havoc in my emotional world. I was the baby sister among the three girls in the family, Susan, the eldest, Bonnie, the second child, and myself. There was a five-year difference between myself and Bonnie, and a 10-year difference between Susan and myself. My mother was a stay-at-home mom, while my father was a self-employed butcher.

Talking of my sisters who shaped my psyche in their own distinct ways, I would first mention Susan. Susan was like a little mother to me. I have pictures of her pushing me in my stroller when I was a baby. She was ten years old, but looked much older. She left to attend college in Boston when I was about 10 years old. I saw her on her visits to Portland, her home. So, my memories of Susan are mostly from when I became an adult. I saw her as both a pretty woman and a tough individual with a strong Boston accent, who personified the core idea of "rugged individualism" for me. She has been very assertive all her life and is still very motherly towards me. She is very neat and tidy and wishes I would be like her. In addition, she has a great sense of humor. Bonnie is a very pretty and popular woman who has always allowed me to hang out with her and her friends. She is talented and adept at almost any craft. A gifted pianist, Bonnie has a lovely, animated personality and is fun to be with. We three siblings got along well, and our age difference helped us avoid sibling rivalry.

My mother kept busy deep cleaning our house and playing golf and tennis, she was a natural athlete. She was there for our basic needs, like cooking dinner and making sure we had nice clean clothes, but she fell short when it came to emotional intelligence, or when it came to gauging any of my deep, emotional needs. When I look back at the days spent in her presence, the predominant memories were of her anger and resentment. She was often raging at my father for one thing or another. She came across as a very unhappy woman, though at that age we didn't understand the root cause of her discontentment.

The memories of my father remain pleasant though. He had also been a standout athlete in his earlier years. My father always provided what we needed, and more. He was the hardest worker I have ever known. In addition to running his own business and doing his own accounting and advertising, he would do all the hard work of a butcher: move sides of beef, bone chickens, cut pork chops, carve other cuts of beef, and clean the shop which meant washing all his equipment to USDA (United States Department of Agriculture) standards. It was a very physical job which would have exhausted anyone else, but he did it all with utmost perfection. All of this occurred while going in and out of the freezer and the deep freezer. He would wake up in the dark at 4 a.m., go to work, and then come home and do the bookwork after supper. The immense stamina and energy with which he worked for decades left me in awe.

I worked for him one summer at his shop when I was a teen. I could not take the cold of the freezers, and he didn't let me get near the hamburger grinder which was the only thing that interested me. So, I never went back to his shop to work in the summers that followed, but I helped him with his bookkeeping in the evenings at the house and was happy with that arrangement. We always ate dinner together as a family in our lovely ranch house and I have beautiful memories of those times. Our yard had flowerbeds and mowed grass, looking like a Norman Rockwell painting; but things were not perfect when it came to our emotional worlds.

As my mother grew older, she started to exhibit her odd and unnatural behavior towards me and my achievements, my milestones. Somehow, I felt I could never please her, no matter how hard I tried. As the days passed by, she would frequently yell at me, and I learned to defend myself by yelling back. She just had to be "right" and yelling was the most pertinent way for her to establish that, but as a young person back then, I did not recognize that she had narcissistic traits, and looking back, I think that also in a way, shaped my emotional being.

My father was a passive kind of guy, and he would never protect me from her frequent episodes of belittling me, though he said he was going to, when we talked in private. I often felt betrayed by him, looking at this dichotomy in his behavior towards me. He was a tough business owner in his work life, but he was an enabler in our home, within our family. If he could not protect himself from my mother's nightly rages at the dinner table, how could he protect me, his offspring?

My mother was the proverbial monkey on my back, and I was petrified of her outbursts. She seemed extremely self-centered to us. She had few boundaries. She would have intense arguments at the dinner table with my father, not thinking those arguments should have been done in private. She would belittle my father in front of us three girls. My losses became her losses in any activity I was involved with. After I finished a tennis match, I would have to hear her tell me how inept I was if I lost. On the other hand, if I won any match she would behave as if she was jealous of my victory. She was enmeshed with me, and had difficulty seeing me as my own person. One time she told me; it was because of her good genes that I won the tournament, a comment which irritated and annoyed me to no end. That day, even if I won physically, I felt like a loser in my mind! I became scared of losing tennis matches because of this dynamic, with the possibility of such harsh behavioral outbursts from my mother. It took away a lot of the joy of playing from my young mind.

The same behavioral outbursts occurred with my mother, when it came to my piano lessons. My mother would sit in on my lessons and if the teacher said negative things, she would harp on it for the whole ride home, and she would continue doing that during the week before the next lesson. Gradually, as the whole affair went on in the same pattern, over the years, I realized that I hated playing the piano due to this dynamic, and I eventually quit when I turned old enough to make my own decisions and I never looked back.

It was so relieving to have my mother off my back when I went away to college at the age of eighteen. It became like a quiet snow storm in my brain whereby the flakes looked big, like they would not accumulate in my head, unlike my mother's constant criticism which often came to a boil in my emotional life. I was free of the monkey on my back, now I just had to learn how to get my internal chatter down from what I parroted internally from my mother. In doing so, I slowly matured with time, and eventually came to see that there were some good things in my childhood that I learned from my mother. When I look back now, I appreciate the tennis lessons and the money and effort she spent on giving them to me. Tennis gave me a lot of joy, a lot of friends, a lot of discipline, a lot of memories, and for that I am grateful. Slowly I was learning how to soothe myself, and rid myself of my mother's negativity. However, this took a great deal of time and effort, and later cost me a lot of money for therapy.

We had interesting times, too. Since my father was a butcher, we ate like royalty. My mother could just call him and say, "Bring home a prime rib and a few rib-eye steaks." When I was really young and uninitiated, I had no idea that most people did not eat like that. Therefore, while my friends ate hamburger helper, I ate like a queen.

Having suffered from bipolar illness for a large chunk of my life, I came to eventually understand that this illness, or any other kind of mental illness is not the fault of one's parent/s, though some traces of the illness can be inherited from any of them. Perhaps if my mother had been more empathetic towards me in my daily life, I would be more able to soothe myself amid my trying times, but I still would have bipolar disorder. Throughout my life, I have experienced the pain of the BEAST as an invincible, uncontrollable force. It completely feels biological. The pain feels like brain pain, for it is excruciating in its own horrible way. Even the best parenting in the world would not have stopped this emotionally ravaging pain. The reality of it is entirely different from what people who have never experienced it think it would be like. Since they don't know the difficult phases, the nuances and the complexities of the disease, they advise us to "think good thoughts". If we could do that, if "thinking good thoughts" would be enough of a remedy, or easily attainable, we wouldn't be in the messy world of depression.

My sister Bonnie had a belief that it was she who caused my bipolar disorder when we were kids. One day, many years back, we kids were horsing around the stairs that led me to tumble down accidentally. I banged my head loudly on the basement floor and started screaming, and my father came running to scoop me up and chastise my sister. It was a very faint memory in my brain, but many years after I got sick, I remember a conversation whereby Bonnie confessed that she thought she triggered my illness from that accidental fall when I was a 4-year-old toddler.

Thereafter, I read many relevant books and literature on the subject, and came to know that many theories abound about the cause of bipolar disorder. However, the fact is, it remains a neurotransmitter dysfunction in the brain which is why medicine is so important. To date I have asked myself what had really triggered my tryst with bipolar disorder, what I could have done differently to have escaped its demons.

My Dad and his three daughters

My parents at a family gathering

During my school days, or in my formative years, I was a busy preteen taking piano lessons, tennis lessons, playing on in the school basketball team, and trying to maintain decent grades. It was the same throughout high school. I became a standout All State basketball player, Most Valuable Player (MVP), and co-captain of my basketball team in high school.

Those were the times when I achieved significant milestones in my school years, which boosted my confidence, my self-esteem and made me content with myself. I won the Maine High School State Singles Championship in tennis in my senior year, and I won an award in a musical competition when I was seventeen, I played a Beethoven Sonata on the piano that earned me a trip to New York City. It was exciting to be in the big city, which dwarfed my hometown, and made me realize there was so much more to the world. I was proud of my achievement, and this trip made me more appreciative of how my mother had instilled discipline by making me practice, even though it annoyed the hell out of me. I became more mature from my trip, by not being so self-centered. I was also awarded Athlete of the Year in my senior year of high school and worked at an ice cream restaurant. I had a busy social life. I was an average student, but I received a lot of attention due to my high athletic and musical achievements, and I was quite happy. My future looked so very bright.

My success continued in my freshman year of college. My first year of college was a blast. I met so many wonderful people and still remember my freshman year with fondness. I was on my own for the first time in my life, and I liked my newfound sense of freedom. I went to the University of Maine, at Orono. I made friends in the dormitory almost instantly; I liked my roommates and hanging around with them was great fun. Also, since I played tennis and basketball I made more friends. My success with athletic achievements continued throughout that period, though around that time, I started to experience some anxiety while in bed before falling asleep. I would worry about major and minor stressors in my life, I worried excessively about my grades and thought I would flunk out. I had trouble sleeping, as I would ruminate about my excessive anxiety. There did not seem to be any trigger for my anxiety, I now think the BEAST was sneaking into my psyche. I was a nervous wreck, but I kept it to myself.

To cope with my anxiety I consumed a lot of alcohol that year, and I wondered if the amount of alcohol I drank in college affected the workings of my brain, hence, the subsequent bipolar illness and anxiety. I came to know from various sources and readings that severe mental illness usually breaks out in the late teens/early twenties, triggered by various significant factors, especially problems with the neurotransmitters in one's brain. I am sure the alcohol I binged on during my college days did not help my brain, and I have concerns if that alone contributed to my disease in some way, though I am not sure. Nevertheless, I still persevered despite my developing anxiety, which I thought was in its nascent stage. I had the hope of getting cured, and that hope has been with me for 41 years now.

Despite my anxiety, I managed to win the Maine Intercollegiate Tennis championship that year, and I started having a relationship with a good-looking, student baseball player. However, around the same time, when my personal, emotional life and my student life seemed to be in equilibrium apparently, the illness started crawling into my mind and soul silently, surreptitiously. I was becoming more and more anxious about the everyday happenings of my life. On the surface level, I appeared fine, fully functional. That explains why not a soul around me could gauge my anxiety, my real disposition, but as I said, I was a wreck from within. I just drank more beer to help squelch whatever was brewing in my brain.

24

And the drinking, unfortunately, only served to fuel my anxiety. The real transition happened during my sophomore year, when my anxiety was becoming problematic, interfering with my daily life. I was anxious about nearly everything. Yet, I must say it was nothing like it became years later when the illness matured. I was still able to cope with the pressures of my daily life as a sophomore, until I lost in the first round in the Maine Intercollegiate Tennis Championship. My mind was racing with unexplained anxiety during the whole match, and the idea of me losing was destroying my confidence. I was starting to feel unhinged.

feated, 6-4, 6-1

Cohen Seizes Schoolgirl Tenn

N PUTNEY
f Writer

High senior, added the sta
e doubles crown she capture
fantgirls by dethroning Sout
in Saturday, 6-4, 6-1;
r home courts, Cohen weave
nts for second set domination
fective with a drop shot tha
k court, where Terri is strong
 strategy successful, but Pam'
rate, her volleying steady and
avenged a 1977 6-2, 6-1 semifin
o indicated by the score.
ces in the surprisingly bris
serves, which she termed us

ged the spin on Pam's dro
tch up to the soft over-the-net
in play.
by Pam and Coach Don Atkin
for the event that attracted a
om 16 schools, worked well
Buckley.
nior, took the No. 2 seed spot
he couldn't solve the superb
ntched in a semifinal match.

mate Robbins in the other
ded No. 10, had ousted No. 4
, 6-0, 6-3; in the fourth round,
Edward Little 3-6, 6-3, 7-6 (5-7
finals.
t for third place, 6-3, 6-2.
the sister of Portland dentist
ew England amateur golfing
captained LHS football and

he Maine summer net circuit,
e state for girls 16 and under
obie Blackwood's LHS squad

To Page 12B

Terri Curtin, right, frequently misjudged the
spin on Pam Cohen's dropshots, and when
she did catch up to the soft over-the-net tap
seldom kept the return in play.
(Staff Photo By John Patriquin)

A glimpse of the Interscholastic State Championship match, featured in a local newspaper. I remember being nervous, but very focused throughout the match.

Pam Cohen of Deering won the state girls singles
tennis crown

This photo is one of my fondest memories when I was competing in high school basketball. That's me, #22, stealing the ball and going in for the layup.

Socially I did well that year. I joined a sorority, and became Pledge Class President. I also started going to fraternity parties with my new friends and I became a binge drinker. It seemed impossible to stop drinking once I started, as I seemed to have little or no control over my urges. It was like my illness, I couldn't control those urges just like I couldn't control the forces in my mind. My friends and I would black out at parties and the next day we would have to fill each other in about what we did the night before. I was lucky I never had alcohol poisoning, but having said that, I sure did have hangovers that were brutal. However, those painful hangovers stopped me from binge drinking. During this phase, I could hardly keep my grades in the "C" range, as the anxiety disorder which I had, started manifesting and my performance in college was compromised. I lived just off campus in a campus-housing complex, where six students lived in each apartment. It was a fun time as my boyfriend lived with his five friend's right across the yard from me. Several apartment units were filled with friends, and there was always a party. As this was happening, I started to feel the adverse effects of my mental illness more and more. I started feeling a sense of separation from other people, no matter how close they were to me, and I became afraid of losing my mind. The anxiety I felt did not feel like your average nervousness/fearfulness. It was a monstrous feeling that made me feel like I absolutely could not cope. It felt as if I were having a nervous breakdown, even though that is just a colloquialism as ones nerves do not break down. I now know that was a sign of an impending mental illness. My brain was getting sick, and I didn't know what to do about it. However, in spite of the vulnerable bouts of anxiety that overwhelmed me during this phase, I never went to the counseling center for treatment, I just blamed the binge drinking and my brutal hangovers for the anxiety and other strange and mysterious feelings. The necessity of it just did not occur to me back then. I thought I was just sad and depressed that so many of my close friends were going to graduate that year, while I would be left alone. I was fearful for my future as I was left behind, and the vulnerability of the situation seeped into my whole being. I became increasingly unable to focus my attention on my studies. I had to finally quit school because the illness became too overwhelming. I could not concentrate.

The experts call the time before onset of a severe mental illness, the "prodromal phase." I strongly believe my sophomore year was that time for me when an insidious and severe mental illness was deepening its roots inside of my brain. I was scared, but I had no name, no explanation for what was happening deep within me, and also, I had no idea that I could be mentally ill. 'This will all work out,' I told myself, assuring myself that I would be okay.

However, it didn't and I never felt normal ever since.

Chapter Two: The BEAST is Identified

Today, 41 years later, I am still a person who suffers from bipolar disorder. My brain does not work properly, but it is all the more difficult as others cannot see it or gauge it like one would gauge a gaping wound or a fractured bone. One may see it manifested in my behavior in various ways. But for the most part, it is invisible to others, like most mental illnesses are. One cannot see it on an X- ray, or a PET scan, or a blood test, or an MRI. It can only be diagnosed through interaction with mental health experts, psychiatrists, and people who are trained specifically to deal with such acute, illnesses. The pain is more intense and seething than one can imagine. That is why suicide attempts or suicide is sometimes its companion, seemingly the only way out of the terrible, unexplained agony. The pain is hard to describe, or even decipher from the surface level. It is not like a headache, but it is a searing, unremitting, agonizing brain pain. It is like intense grief with a terrible self-loathing component to it. It influences my mood in an oppressive negative direction while it interferes with my sense of emotional balance. The pain is blinding in its own monstrous way. It is hard to understand its nuances, unless one has had it, and one would know it if they had a major depressive episode any time in his/her life.

Depression is a liar, a thief in the night that steals one's true self. I am not the same when I am having one of those terrible bouts of depression. My thoughts churning in the deep recesses of my mind tell me I am fat, ugly, worthless, incapable, unlovable, insensitive, uncaring and thoughtless. When I am in a depression, I am incapable of feeling either concern or love from anybody else in the world. For whatever reason, this 'brain chemistry gone awry' does not allow any room for connection with others, nor does it allow me to feel empathy or compassion from them. No external stimuli can help me during that terribly daunting phase. I am absolutely alone, like a secluded island. A beautiful day when the depression hits me makes me feel more intensely alone as it is so contrary to how I feel. The pain is unrelenting, and all I can say is that this unrelenting pain of depression has been my constant companion an unwelcome guest in my head for long periods. I hate depression more than anything I know, except for anxiety, which is her best friend.

With lots of medication and years of recovery, with learning and implementing new coping skills, having peer support and a healthy community, sticking with a therapist and a psychiatrist, my illness now comes and goes like a troubled relationship that I cannot get out of.

It is not as bad as it used to be. For the first fifteen years of having it, I went without the intervention of psychiatric medication. My synapses and neurotransmitters were tumbling, destroying everything in their paths, like a tornado.

As I mentioned earlier, my illness started when I was 19. I was waitressing for the summer when this ungodly, unexplainable pain came over me. It was something that I had never experienced before in any form. The pain rattled me to my core, and while I was dealing with its onslaughts, part of me knew this would be a long journey. It was as if my soul knew it would stay with me somehow. So, I ran out of the restaurant that day, about two miles to my family home. My mother was visiting my uncle during that time, so I went to the basement and waited for him to leave. When he left, I told my mother that something was terribly, terribly wrong with me. Due to my sudden confession, she became somewhat puzzled, but at the same time, she was unable to understand my problems or comfort me. However, she did make a call to a medical center and got appointments with a therapist and psychiatrist for me. I remember I saw some older woman therapist, who, upon hearing I had a boyfriend, assumed I was worried about being pregnant. I knew that was far from being the truth, and that was not even the problem. But somehow, she did not seem to believe me. Hence, this was the beginning of my journey to recovery, whatever that meant; I did not have a clue. The psychiatrist told me to seek help elsewhere as I was moving to Texas in a few weeks. He refused to give me medication because I guess he was not sure what underlying psychological issues I was dealing with. He just did not have enough information for treating me after only one visit.

After my sophomore year in college, I quit school and I could no longer feel anything for my boyfriend. The depression took away my ability to connect with him on any level, so I moved home to live with my parents. However, even there, during my regular interactions with them, I realized that no one seemed to know how to help me. I did not have a clue how to help myself. At the age of 19, I was inarticulate, and unable to ask for help. Who would, under such circumstances, and also, at such a tender age? I grew deeply ashamed of myself, as my illness began to lay down its roots. Shame and fear were at the heart of my illness. I made it through those days, months, and years with sheer willpower.

I often contemplated about the possibility of suicide during that phase, but I never planned it. I was too afraid of not succeeding, and the stigma that came with it. In those days, I exercised like a fiend, and I believe that kept me functioning. In addition, the "rugged individualism" with which I grew up in Portland, my hometown, helped me keep my nose to the grindstone and persevere. However, the pain persisted in spite of my best efforts to evade it, to keep it at bay. This mystifying brain pain was a BEAST.

Living with my parents was becoming increasingly difficult day by day. I had extended family and many friends around, but I felt detached from all of them. I stopped talking about the agony after some time because my malfunctioning brain reprimanded me silently, making me feel ashamed. With everything I did, I felt I was being a burden to them. After all, why couldn't I snap out of it? I bought into the stigma of the times. After all, I was feeling so burdened that I projected this burden onto them.

After about a year, I decided to go back to school, and move to West Texas, where my sister Bonnie and brother-in-law Matt were living at that time. I went to Texas Tech University in Lubbock, Texas where Matt was a law student and my sister was a Head Resident in an all-girls dormitory. The cost was cheap, and I felt that at least my life would have some meaning and structure once I was settled there. However, I moved to Lubbock and experienced a culture shock as things I saw there were so different from what I had seen all along in Maine. In the seventies, I wore jeans, tennis shoes and shirts. The young women at Tech wore clothes befitting of a beauty pageant just to go to class. I felt like a fish out of water.

During my undergraduate days, life became all the more difficult. In order to get in-state tuition at four dollars a credit hour, I had to work 20 hours a week for the University, so I took a job in the cafeteria. It was during this phase that my brain pain was the most excruciating, but I had to somehow go through the daily rigmarole of life, just so that I could survive. Waking up to have breakfast and go to work in the early mornings seemed a huge task for me. My agony was and always has been the worst in the mornings.

But somehow the job I used to do back in those days became the reason of my survival. My day job provided me with mindless work and a structure or routine, which helped me function on an everyday basis. I was a functioning depressed individual. I have never had a migraine headache, but having depression always made me compare my condition to having blinding migraine pain. I related the migraine analogy to the incapacitating pain I was feeling during my bouts of depression and mania.

I then put all my energies and efforts into my studies, whereas my focus had been on my social life before all this happened. I started racking up the A's, so on the outside I looked successful, enterprising and composed, with a part-time job and a 3.5 grade point average. Not bad. However, deep within, I was still having this gnawing feeling that I was a burden to everyone, just by being alive. It was during this period when I was offered the position of a supervisor in the cafeteria. I felt that I had fooled them into believing I was worthy, and that I deserved an academy award for my continued performance of appearing as "Happy Pam."

Chapter Three: The Beast Confronts the Therapist

Finally, I decided to reach out for help. I began to see a therapist once a week at the University's counseling center. Neither she nor I ever discussed being evaluated by a psychiatrist. Back in those days as I stated earlier, psychodynamic or Freudian therapy was quite the rage, consisting of making the unconscious conscious. Back in those days, it also meant they blamed your mother for your upbringing. That fit well for me, as my mother and I were often bitter foes. I came to love my therapist and my sessions with her. I could finally talk to someone about the misery I was experiencing, and she was as kind as she could be as she listened to my anguish week after week. I would daydream about the next session because I looked so forward to them. However, when she decided to dig into my past I would become more morose. Sadly, the therapy sessions with the therapist did nothing to help my depression. On the contrary, it made it worse. My agony was largely biological, and bringing up the pain which was pent up inside me since long ago overwhelmed me.

My therapist did not know what to do with me, so she pawned me off to an intern named Stuart. However, I had formed a bond with her through these sessions, though she didn't seem to know the way to help me. Stuart was a nice person, but he did not offer me anything new in reducing my pain. Now I had the grief of losing the therapist, one of the very few persons I was connected to. I was heartbroken. She was like a mother to me and losing contact with her, I felt untethered and lost. I still felt worthless, unlovable, insensitive, uncaring, and ugly to my core as negative emotions ensued from the depression. I thought I could not bear the brain pain any longer, but somehow, I endured.

During this phase, I graduated from Texas Tech Magna Cum Laude, but to get there was a grind, for I had to reread my assignments over and over because I was so distracted from my inner turmoil. After graduation I moved back to Maine with my parents since I had no money. After a few months of aimless desperation, I went to work for an optometrist, though I knew nothing about eyes. I moved into an apartment with two friends who were nurses. In retrospect, when I think about those days, I remember one of my co-workers complaining that she felt I did not listen to her when she confided in me. I was clearly unable to concentrate and she clearly saw it as an indication that something was wrong with me. From my personal experience, a depressed brain is a busy brain. I was often distracted and had to multitask, balancing my inner pain with the external world and its multiple demands.

This same co-worker later encouraged me to become a tennis teaching professional. I myself was confident that I had the skill set, I just needed to learn how to effectively teach the game. Therefore, I went and became certified as a Professional Tennis Teaching Professional from the USPTR (United States Professional Tennis Registry). Thereafter I got a job at the indoor tennis/fitness club where I had grown up working, taking lessons, and practicing. Initially I was happy that it was a great milestone in my career and thought for a while that it would enhance my mental health too.

However, soon after, I began having panic attacks in addition to my depression. Nevertheless, for fifteen years I successfully taught tennis, and I would be amazed at how I managed to do that amid the great agony which was killing me from inside. I became a great actress as I learned to hide my agony from the outside world. My panic attacks came in the form of depersonalization. In that state, I felt detached from my body and my voice seemed to originate from somewhere outside of me. I had a horrible sense of dread that I could not shake away. I would have this while saying tennis instructions, things like "watch the ball" or "hit through the ball more." As I went on with my daily life, camouflaging my pain every single day, my ability to deal with both the real world and my internal agony, two diametrically opposing worlds surprised me; it was an incredibly lonely experience. Once again, I was alone with the crazy volcano in my head that I rarely told anyone about. Finally, after a lot of tribulations and anguish in my private, inner world, I went to another therapist. I do not remember learning anything useful for my illness, but at least I had an outlet, someone to complain to, to vent out about my pain. In those sessions too, the 'mother issues' evolved once again. Repeatedly, I complained about my mother to the therapist. Due to the intense nature of those sessions which brought to the surface our pent-up agony and anguish, I began to believe that my mother was the root cause of this unbearable pain in my head. The therapy was once again unhelpful, and made me more vulnerable.

Then, my illness took a darker turn. I began having delusions, bordering on religious thoughts and allusions. I thought I was the second coming of Christ, an interesting delusion for a Jewish girl. I would drive with my eyes closed because I thought if I really were Jesus, I would not need my eyes, for I believed I had super powers. I once tried to poke my eyes out, until the pain made me nauseated and I vomited. In this state of utter pain and psychosis, I thought that I had suffered like Jesus and was chosen for this. What I did not understand was that I was very sick and needed medicine to prevent these excruciating symptoms of suffering. I was delusional for an entire year, thinking of all crazy and irrational possibilities. When I told my therapist all of this, she sent me to a therapist who was also a psychic. This therapist/ psychic told me I was having a spiritual awakening that was happening too fast. She thought I had a chakra problem. I believed that my chakras were flooding me. Whatever a chakra really was? I thought it was some New Age phenomenon that was going to analyze my pain and suffering from a spiritual standpoint and alleviate it all in the process. My original therapist put me in group therapy where I made a fool out of myself for several months talking nonsense. This craziness went on and on.

Finally, I got lucid enough to seek out another therapist. Her name was Deidre, and she told me I had problems which could be called 'psychotic'. She told me she knew my delusions might have appeared real to me, but they were in fact, not true. It was a relief and a crushing blow all at once. In my deluded mind, I have to admit I liked the idea of feeling special like Jesus, but, at the same time, when I realized it was all the delusional workings of my mind, the pressure was off. Being Jesus is a big job after all! I never saw a psychiatrist, nor was one recommended to me. I think my external persona that I used to function in society got in the way of seeing me as sick as I was, Therefore, I think the therapists and psychologists thought they could fix me with their theories and their therapies alone, hence no need to see a psychiatrist. Plus, they all thought I had unipolar depression, not bipolar disorder. I got out of that psychotic world with time and a therapist who had good reality testing. The right medications would have gotten me out of it much more quickly. I should have been in the hospital, but the circumstances were not conducive to making it happen.

When my psychosis abated, I went to the Portland School of Massage Therapy and became a massage therapist. The structure of the classes and the work helped me function, and this job helped to soothe my body and mind, for giving a massage quieted my anxiety. I had become burned out, teaching tennis for years. With massage therapy, I had the benefit of getting the relaxation response using focused attention, and relaxing music. I practiced massage therapy at two different fitness clubs. I also received a lot of massages which I would trade with other practitioners. That also was helpful for my mental state. I did that for eight years, until my body was too tired to continue. I now have carpal tunnel syndrome from all that physical work giving massages, and hitting tennis balls for so long.

I remained in therapy with Deidre for about 5 years, and then had to discontinue meeting with her. The end of our relationship came when I met a man, eventually fell in love, and moved with him to Maryland where he got a job. My grieving for Deidre did not sit lightly on my heart. I missed her greatly. It is hard to tell your inner secrets to someone, only to know your heart may be broken in the end. But one does not hang out with one's therapist when therapy is over; it is unprofessional after all. It is final no matter which side decides to end it. That is the way it is. Grief is the by-product, a necessary loss. In this ordeal of losing touch with a trusted confidante, the grief was heavy and abiding, and it took quite a while for me to cope with the loss.

Chapter Four: The BEAST and Relationships; Me, Him and my Illness

Relationships have always been hard work for me, whether they are therapeutic or romantic. Joe was the first man I had ever lived with. There were three of us in the relationship, me, him and my illness. I had met Joe at the tennis facility I was working at. He was also a teaching tennis professional from out of state who had come to Maine to visit a mutual friend of ours. Joe had a lot of nice qualities. He was a good critical thinker with a sharp mind. Both of us were ranked highly in tennis, and were independent, so we were compatible with each other in many ways. In our daily life together, I hid a lot of my illness from him, because my shame and stigma related to my illness didn't let me open up to him fully. Also, I was myself in a fix about the origin of the pain from my bipolar disorder. I would often try to figure out where the pain was coming from, and not having much of a clue, I was lost and dismayed. Though I knew that the pain was largely biological, I would sometimes blame Joe, because he was there. He was tangible. My anger outbursts were quite serious. I would threaten to leave the relationship. Because of the BEAST, I was irritable and I could not let things blow over. In my past, my mother often threatened for the family to go to counseling where she thought she would be seen as "right" and would feel vindicated; I guess I picked up that behavior from her. I always thought I was right! Joe was also very much a loner, and he had his share of problems too. After about five years of being together, I left the relationship. I moved a lot after my break-up and the agony that resulted deep within me followed. Due to my mania and ruminating thoughts that defined that phase, I reasoned that the pain would be better if only I would go somewhere new. At that time, I had a lot of energy. I was manic.

I certainly was not cured from my depression when I left Deidre, but, to her credit, she guided me out of my make belief world, my psychosis. For me, being psychotic was somewhat entertaining, stimulating, as well as hugely terrifying because in that state I was so out of touch with reality. Fortunately, even in that vulnerable state, I had an observing ego that watched out for the other part of me at times. My observing ego was my saner self, who would sometimes make me think that my psychotic ideas were, in fact crazy. At other times, my observing ego would not be there, and in her absence, I would believe my delusions and become anxious, agonized, and obsessive.

My grandiose delusion took over my life, and I also felt some powerful external force was taking over my body. I would rotate in circles while in the shower until I almost fell down from dizziness. It might sound crazy to many people, but I felt compelled to do this. I would hallucinate and see colors around people and objects, usually the color green. Moreover, my brain would process this and try to make meaning out of it, though there was no meaning to make. The BEAST was omnipresent. I still was depressed and feeling all the worthlessness and anhedonia (lack of pleasure) that the BEAST dished out. Only now I had the stimulation of the delusions and hallucinations that actually strengthened the illness. The mood swings and emotional outbursts were so dramatic and unprecedented that I would go from grandiose to worthless at the drop of a hat. I also did not get much sleep. In retrospect, I think this was my first mixed episode of depression and mania together, though Deidre insisted it was psychosis from my depression. This diagnosing business is very tricky, for many brain illnesses can present themselves very similarly. Psychosis is a common symptom of many mental illnesses. It is like the term "fever" that signals a physical illness is present. The definition and analysis of psychosis which I learnt from Deidre indicated that something had gone haywire in the brain. And I was silently, anxiously witnessing this debilitating pain as my brain was becoming a ravaged mess.

My quest to get help for my depression continued. In Maryland, I saw my first psychiatrist. He gave me a tricyclic antidepressant and a book entitled, "Primal Scream." Neither the book nor the antidepressant worked. I also began seeing another therapist. I cannot recall her name or what she looked like. I just remember the psychiatrist was kind, and looked like a stereotypical psychiatrist with unkempt hair and small eye glasses. The reason the antidepressant and the book did not work is because I was misdiagnosed with MDD. Antidepressants alone most times, make a person who really has bipolar disorder, manic, or cause a mixed episode. That wasn't common knowledge in those days.

Despite my desperation for healing, I also knew I needed structure. I got a job at a YMCA in Bowie, Maryland, where I had been working out. I started as a trainer in the fitness room. I was working full-time at the YMCA and now opening the facility for the 6 am workout fanatics. It was a great job except I had to get up at 5 a.m. The worst time when the BEAST was in its most active phase, once again. However, the job was pretty stress- free, so the BEAST became quieter eventually, and the pain went from an eight to a six on a scale of 1-10. I also was exercising during that phase, which also helped keep me calm.

It was during those days that I decided to enroll in graduate school. I applied for my Master's Degree at Loyola College in Baltimore. I planned to study clinical psychology. Part of me thought I would figure out the clinical aspect of my disease, as I was still not realizing that I had a malfunctioning brain and not a character disorder. I needed medicine nonetheless, but these tricyclic's did not work for my body. Once again I now realized that I could be writhing in agony from inside and yet not let it show. I was so used to playing "Happy Pam." Out of my mouth came words of torment, yet my exterior looked and sounded normal. It was a survival mechanism which I had learned over the years. I must have been confusing for the doctors to assess my real condition, for I was able to function, though in tremendous pain

So, I worked the morning shift at the YMCA then drove an hour to Baltimore, where I took two classes a semester until I earned my degree. I would also like to add here that I was appalled at the content of some of my classes. In the 1990's, old theories of psychological disorders were hard to dismiss, even as the medical model was becoming more pre-dominant. One theory of mania was that it was a "flight from depression." What utter nonsense! I thought to myself. If I could have switched to mania or more accurately hypomania, a milder form of mania, I would have jumped at the chance. It surely would be better than the depression I was feeling. I guess one was supposed to magically switch from depression to mania by some sort of happenstance, but I did not know what that was. The BEAST loved this theory, and I could feel her use it against me, "see you do this to yourself, you're so inept that you can't even get hypomanic/manic."

Thinking of the content of my coursework, and especially the way mental illnesses were explained in the texts I studied, I felt hopeless and started questioning if I should continue with my studies. Some of the psycho-diagnostics techniques were also laughable. We would analyze one's drawing of a human figure and or a tree. It was ridiculous to give meaning to things that had no meaning; and it reminded me of my psychosis, as there were no critical thinking skills involved. I felt ashamed that this is where my field was during the late 1990's. Nevertheless, I still did not recognize that I had a brain illness, at least not formally, though it felt like one. I constantly fought with the BEAST within me, thinking all the while that this agony had been due to a weak character. After all, that was the message I was getting from the therapists treating me, and now in school too, that those of us with "mental illness" somehow inflict this pain upon ourselves. Even when I was fighting back those skewed theories, trying to find more pertinent explanations, I was just confused. It was a 'blame the victim' theory and culture that was propagated everywhere. It still largely is.

My favorite classes in graduate school were my statistics classes. I learned to become a better critical thinker. You could not just believe any theory that sounded interesting, you had to reject the null hypothesis, or fail to reject it, meaning that things had high probability of being true or little to no probability of being true. Stat classes fortified my 'observing ego'. The hardest part about my serious, acute brain illness was that my thoughts while in my depressed state, were often untrue, or deeply skewed in one direction. My consciousness about my own self-worth was perpetually in a negative direction. Due to those uncontrollable, obsessive negative thoughts, I felt so miserable about so many areas of my life. Having come a long way from those days, I now view the illness of my depression as a reality disorder. The critical thinking which I learned during those days did not cure me from my negative ruminations, but it definitely endowed me with some insight. If I were to test my negative thoughts against the probability that they were in fact not true, I could at least know that my negative thoughts were not accurate much of the time. However, I could not change those thoughts when depressed. It was only when medicine started helping me that I could use this cognitive therapy as a coping skill, not a cure. Living with this illness for such a long time, I have come to realize that there is no cure, only the management of symptoms. A bitter pill to swallow.

I was very lonely and tired most of the time, but at the same time, there was this silent, yet strong desire to have a romantic relationship, to try loving someone again. I began looking at personal ads in the newspaper. This was long before computer dating sites were prevalent. I went out on a couple of dates, whereby nothing much happened. I tried dating again after a short hiatus and that was when I met Tim. I thought he was attractive, nice and attentive in his behavior. I could tell he liked me, and I was impressed by him. We began dating. Over time I divulged much more information to him about my feelings and my illness, as he was very kind and patient. One day he asked me if he could tell his parents that I had bipolar disorder because he felt that they would want to help me if they could. His sincere concern for me and his request to help me took away a little of the stigma I always had, and that itself was a great help. I thought that maybe it was okay to reach out for help, and that maybe there were people who would try to understand situations like mine.

After about a year of dating, Tim and I moved in together. As is often the case, it was fabulous in the beginning, but once again there were three of us in the relationship; me, him and my illness. I would get annoyed and yell at him, and threaten to leave him, just like I did in my previous relationship. On his part, he was a caregiver by nature, but was quite needy. He did not have good boundaries when I needed space, and no matter how much I talked with him about it, nothing ever changed. It was during this phase when I was still with him that I got really manic one time and cheated on him. He was willing to forgive me, but at that time, I knew in my mind that it was over. I did not come out of that episode of mania for a long time, and during the entire time, I was hypersexual. In that manic state, I had a lot of short-term relationships after Tim and I broke up, and I also had a very bad sense of judgment about people in general, which landed me in trouble, one after the other.

In the late 1990's I started taking "new" antidepressants, the serotonin re-uptake inhibitors (SSRI's). Prozac was the rage, but it did not offer me much relief. I took a slew of these new meds as they became available in the market. However, as I started to consume them all, I became manic once again. However, I did not recognize my manic state or know for sure that it was the cause of my racing thoughts, my boundless energy, my huge sexual appetite, or my feeling like I was superior to others. Neither did the doctors. At this point in time, the medical community was still not aware that antidepressants make people who are diagnosed with just depression, manic if the underlying condition was really bipolar disorder. At this point I had been with one psychiatrist after another in huge desperation and found them no more helpful than the therapists. I found myself nearly homeless, but I was lucky because my parents bailed me out and paid for me to live in an apartment in Maryland. I was hardly sleeping, drinking pots of coffee a day, and smoking a pack of cigarettes daily. I was a lost self with no goals, no direction whatsoever. I mostly had mixed episodes, whereby I would be depressed and manic at the same time. It was an agitated state that made me feel like I would spontaneously combust.

I was still seeing a psychologist, even though she wasn't really helping me with my enormous and burdensome pain. I was probably very tough to work with, given my agitated state. No amount of talk therapy could soothe me. One night I checked myself into the hospital. I was in the ER for hours before anyone would deal with me. I was in excruciating pain, though I couldn't possibly explain its severity to anyone there. If this had been physical agony, I would have been triaged perhaps to the Intensive Care Unit, but because my pain was psychological, I was ignored. So, as a natural recourse, I started screaming, asking for help, pleading that I couldn't take the pain much longer and needed an injection of Ativan. I created such a stir, that some man from the psychiatric unit was called in to see me. If I had stayed home, I could have taken some clonazepam, a medication for anxiety. In the hospital ER, this screaming and pleading for medications seemed unreasonable to them. Finally, I was given a small dose of Ativan and moved into the psychiatric unit.

At the psychiatric unit, I still felt indescribably agitated, so I found a mat on the floor and put it up against a wall and started punching it. I remember telling the nurse that was watching me do this that I was having a bad day. She began to laugh. I walked up to her and asked with a lot of agitation, "Why are you laughing at me?" She said because I was obviously having a bad day. This infuriated me further. The next thing I recall was that I went somewhere to get a coke. I was alone and took a heavy chair and threw it about an inch out of frustration. Just then, I noticed that a doctor was watching me and I heard her say, "call security". Before I knew it, four people were on me, trying to put me in restraints. I resisted their overtures, asking for a shot of Ativan for the entire time. They took my shirt and bra off of me, which made me feel helpless and violated, and then they handcuffed me to some sort of stretcher. Then, suddenly, I felt a stab in my leg, which is when it occurred to me that they had probably given me a shot of Ativan. I fell asleep for a long time, and when I woke up, I was still in restraints. I couldn't understand why they had not given me the shot when I asked for it, why they chose to deal with me in such a brutal, inhuman way. I would have volunteered for the shot; I was begging them for one. Before I knew it, I was in an ambulance. They shipped me to another hospital, apparently more equipped for volatile patients. I wondered why they did that, because as much as I know or believe, I was sick, and not violent. I did not try to hurt myself when I was punching the mat; that is why I put it against the wall. I was begging for help, to no avail. I had barely thrown a chair in desperation, in agitation. And four people jumped at me immediately after. I had post-traumatic stress symptoms for at least 6 months after this incident.

I awoke to find myself in a locked ward. The fluorescent lights were shining brightly. The people there were scary. Some were in restraints, all of them seemed psychotic. I remember seeing blood but I do not recall where. There were patients behind locked doors, banging on them in an attempt to be freed. Others were locked to stretchers, restrained like I had been. People were loudly talking to themselves and were visibly agitated, some were screaming. It was a circus atmosphere like in the movie "One Flew Over the Cuckoos' nest." that I badly wanted out of. Luckily, I had escaped psychosis. I was terrified, but I also got calmer from the Ativan. A psychiatrist came into see me and thankfully, she immediately got me off of that ward. I was now on a floor where I had freedom to make calls and move about. But, the BEAST in my head would not relent. I was sure this time, I would in fact, spontaneously combust, just disappear into thin air from the pain in my brain, my psyche, my mind, my soul. They put me on some new meds in the hospital and sent me home within that week. I was still very sick, reeling from the aftermath of the tremendous pain of the attack and my emotional pain. One night I called that psychiatrist who let me out of the volatile ward. She was on call. She told me to go to bed and that she would see me in the morning. She admonished me for calling her so late, sarcasm dripping from her voice. The next day she gave me some different pills and sent me on my way. I tried calling her again when the agony hit, and I was also vomiting every fifteen minutes from the high dose of a second generation antipsychotic called Abilify, that she gave me. But she never picked up the phone and only had her answering machine on thereafter.

I eventually got myself a new psychiatrist, a kinder one that I had heard about when I was in the hospital open ward. This new psychiatrist accepted me as her patient, and she was as kind as she was rumored to be. She took a liking to me and made me feel like I was her favorite patient. She kept on changing medicines for me to help alleviate my pain and agony, but nothing seemed to help my depression and my agitated state. It seemed as though I was a rapid cycler, treatment resistant, moving from the depths of despair to outright agitated grandiosity where I felt as if I was a genius. Meanwhile, the psychologist I was seeing in addition to the psychiatrist, must have been more and more discouraged and impatient by my lack of improvement. One day I threw a Kleenex box in her office in an agitated state. After this, she would no longer would see me, which was her choice.

Surprisingly enough, she never gave me a referral to another therapist, which really upset me. I had been her client for about three years and saw her twice weekly. Though she couldn't really help my brain pain, once again I lost a connection, and the grief, with all its denial, anger, bargaining with God to trade my legs for peace of mind, and disappointment, was mine to bear. She called my kind psychiatrist, and as much as I can recall, my psychiatrist conveyed that she had no patience for therapists who abandoned their clients. This ever so compassionate psychiatrist assured me that she would see me through and continue to work with me. I spent my days in a tormented state, just trying to stay alive.

Survival was my new job. I did not want this BEAST in my head to kill me, but the agony was a mighty foe. I couldn't even weep, for I was in too much pain as my brain was tormented all the time. I found another psychologist during this time so that I could have someone to analyze and convey my inner life. It helped with my aloneness. Not that I thought he could help me, although part of me still had hopes for a miracle cure.

My mania took me to Holland where I had met someone virtually on the Internet who lived in Soest, a small city in the Netherlands. I met this person on an online forum that I had started on yahoo.com. I had previously been involved on a computer chat room where I met a woman online who claimed she had lost her husband and two children in a plane crash. After a year or more chatting with her on the online forum she came to visit me in real life. She opined about the loss of her family over and over again. I held space and listened to her grief. After a while I began to get suspicious that her plane crash story may not be true, as her details were becoming sketchy over time. To make a long story short, this person had fooled me. She did not have a husband, nor children, and there was never a plane crash, I was furious. When I calmed down over time I did some research and realized she had something called Factitious Disorder. It's when people lie for attention. It's a lesser form of Munchausen Syndrome whereby people fake sick or make themselves sick for attention. They also tell tall tales, again for attention. So, I started a forum for people who had been duped by someone with this illness. Over time a person from the Netherlands posted on my forum. They had been duped by a person pretending to have cancer. There were over 20 people posting on my site, but this Netherlander posted often and their story resonated with me. Over time, and after many conversations online and on the telephone, I thought I was in love, even though I barely knew this person, so I desired to go to the Netherlands and meet this person. I didn't give a thought to the fact that this online contact could have mislead me to their identity, or that I could have met with more dangerous consequences. My judgment was impaired due to mania, and I forgotten I had just been duped by the woman with factitious disorder. My own safety was the least important concern in my mind during that phase, and my hyper- sexuality was in full bloom. So I was hoping for a sexual encounter. I was lucky that this person was very kind and didn't get me into any trouble. God only knows what mischief I could have gotten my manic self into.

When I came back from Holland I was still drifting, still just trying to survive that inner battle that I was fighting with, and trying to deal with the real world. I re-applied for and was awarded Social Security Disability Benefits. The small sum of just under a thousand dollars a month would be mine to live on. My rent was over eight hundred dollars. And, I would have to wait a year before I was eligible for Medicare health insurance. I had been working as a grief counselor for a hospice in Maryland, but the mania and the mixed episodes made me ask for a leave of absence. Not that my performance was all too great at that time. They said I could come back when I got well, whenever that would be. After five years at that job, it was time for me to move on. But I hadn't a clue where I was moving, or which direction my mind was taking me.

One thing about my mania was that it kept me occupied with my own thoughts. My brain was abuzz with many thoughts and ideas. Once again, I thought I was a genius. I spent most of my time in chat rooms on the computer, and taking some classes in basic computer applications at a community college. I was also trying to get together a documentary on factitious disorder when I wasn't too hypersexual to be looking for a sexual adventure, whether on the phone, in cyberspace, or in real life. Hyper sexuality may sound fun to some extent, but it completely overtook my mind and led me on to unwarranted situations. I was one big walking hormone, and would find others with the same problem!

I finally came back down to earth after I had moved about three times and crashed into a deep mixed episode that led me to the hospital. It was a long time before I had any stability in my life, both physically and emotionally. One day I saw and advertisement in the local newspaper looking for a roommate. I answered the ad. The cost was within my budget and the lady looking for a roommate was also the landlady. She had an adult daughter with a mental illness, so I told her my story. She handled it better than most people due to her experience with her daughter. We hit it off and I moved in with her. I finally found a stable living situation after all of my frenetic moving around from person to person/place to place. Additionally, Tim and I were still friends, and his company helped soothe me. Also, my kind psychiatrist was trying to help me by getting me to try various mood stabilizers, and antipsychotics. Mood stabilizers are mostly anti-seizure medications like Tegretol, Depakote, and Trileptal. Apparently, these anti-seizure medications have been found to help stabilize mood. Unfortunately I was allergic to all of them. However, the anti-psychotic Risperidone did help quite a bit. My pain was lessened but I was still unstable as I kept experimenting with different medications.

I never gave up hope that I could find a medicinal cocktail that would ease my pain, and neither should you!

Chapter Five: Moving, Mania and Mixed Episodes

My trip to Holland scared my family. Eventually they realized how sick I was, and how shitty my judgment was even though they were living in Dallas. At the age of 80, my father came to Maryland to get me to take me back to the "Big D" where he lived with my mother. My two sisters also lived in Garland, Texas, near Dallas. I went kicking and screaming, for I did not want to go back to Texas. I was a liberal Democrat living near Washington D.C. and the thought of going to a conservative state unhinged me. My first experience living in Lubbock, Texas did not produce fond memories. And, as I have already stated before, I didn't get along well enough with my mother. Remember, I was encouraged to think that she was the cause of my problems. My issues with my mother never got resolved at that time, and I cannot tell if either of us made any efforts in that direction. In my case, I didn't have the means to make any efforts then. It was years later when my bipolar illness was much more stable that I was able to tackle my mother issues.

In spite of my strong initial resistance, I moved to Dallas, and in with my parents. It was a disaster. I was seething in deep anger directed at my parents; I hated being forced to make this move in the first place. I was grieving for leaving Maryland, and the independent life I had, no matter how chaotic. I had to leave behind my friends, my community, and the places that were familiar to me. I didn't want to start over in a new city. So, we began to fight. I found myself coming down from mania into the deepest depression of my life. I begged them to kill me, something I didn't have the nerve to try myself. Despite our horrible screaming episodes, I noticed that my agony brought my parents to tears. They would cry when I begged them to kill me. In my mind, though, I was only being logical. My mental state was a mammoth burden to me, that I thought that they were plagued by the same burden themselves. I couldn't connect with the fact that they loved me, and were pained to witness and understand my pain and turmoil. I couldn't see how my illness was really affecting them, I could only see and feel my pain as a deeply personal experience. My pursuit of living in spite of my vulnerable emotional, psychological state seemed utterly hopeless, and so horribly burdensome. I projected my feelings of being trapped on to them. I thought I was better off dead for all of us, and that seemed to me the only remedy to this excruciating situation.

In this anguish I decided to go to the hospital. I stayed there for nearly three months for my psychiatric condition. I had the worst agitated state to date; the deepest and the most painful. I never knew that my illness could get any worse than those days in my past but I was dead wrong. I could barely function. I couldn't bathe; I could hardly get myself dressed for the day. All I wanted to do was escape, but there was no escape, I felt totally trapped in a nightmarish pain. I was hardly responding to the people around me. I went to the hospital, for I was feeling despondent and in deep, incurable agony. I remember people calling me out, "Pam, Pam, Pam", and I was so turned inward that I could hardly respond or deal with the world outside in any way. I wasn't catatonic, but probably the closest thing to it.

During this incredibly painful state of mine, the doctors talked me into getting electroconvulsive shock treatments, (ECT) because other modalities weren't working. I had fourteen ECT treatments. Patients would line up to get on those gurneys where the treatment would take place. They would come from both in the hospital and from home. I, on my part, would lie on a stretcher and wait for the doctor to give me anesthesia. Going under anesthesia, being unconscious was the only thing that brought me some peace, albeit for a few minutes, for getting away from the pain for a bit gave me some relief.

I recall the doctor telling me to "pick out a good thought." Heck, if I would really be able to do that, I might not have been in the predicament I was in. I earnestly prayed that I would die during one of the treatments. I wanted to be let out of this tormenting hell. I would wake up flighty and foggy. My depression never seemed any better in my own mind, however, after several treatments my anger improved, or at least that's what the doctors said. I think I just didn't remember so much about what I was angry about. So, while they saw this as some kind of improvement, I still wanted to be out of the pain. But now my memory was damaged. I couldn't remember much of anything from about the two years prior to my shock treatments. The doctors had warned me about this, but somehow, I didn't feel ready for this.

Eventually I went back to my parent's home and saw a psychiatrist on an outpatient basis. It was one trial medicine after another. I do remember begging her for some kind of medication for my anxiety. However, she resisted saying that she did not want me sleeping all the time. In my utterly vulnerable state, with nothing to calm me down, as well as nothing to stop my worst depression to date, I felt like I was trapped. I didn't even dare to kill myself. With that option off the table, I really felt terrified. What if I had to live my whole life in this kind of pain? I wondered, feeling lost and miserable.

I switched psychiatrists. One thing I am proud of about myself is that I never gave up trying to get some help. When people didn't hear me, I screamed in the ER, when a psychiatrist wouldn't give me medicine for my anxiety, I found one that would. What I learned from these experiences is that those of us with mental illness have to be our own best advocates. Through this arduous journey of this life, I have gathered that no one else can possibly know what we suffer from, what we endure, so we have to tell them in any way we can, and if and when they can't hear us, we move onto someone else who will help us out.

While I was beginning my recovery from this horrible state, my sister Bonnie began an Internet search for group homes for me, so that I could live in human company other than my parents. On one occasion, I tried to live in an apartment, but that lasted one day. Apparently, I could not tolerate living alone even for 24 hours, while on the other hand, I also found living with my parents impossible. My sister found a non-profit organization called PLAN which was an acronym for Planned Living Assistance Network of North Texas. They served and gave emotional support and social recognition to people with severe brain illnesses. I immediately liked that they referred to mental illness as a form of brain illness, because I knew all along that is what I had. I knew my brain was disrupted, impaired. So, I was amenable to go for an interview to see what they had to offer me, if anything. We met with a woman named Paula, the Executive Director, who was also a Licensed Clinical Social Worker. Despite their differences with me, my family accompanied me. Paula told me there was an apartment complex across the street that she could connect me with. Moreover, I would be able to walk to Iris Place, a place where they had educational and social activities for people with SMI, which was an added attraction for me. Hence, I discovered I would have a place to go during the daytime, while having the opportunity to live independently. The thought of living independently gave me hope that I could get back on track with my life. I thought it was time to try.

I moved into a very small apartment near Iris Place. The BEAST and I coexisted again, but now I could take the two of us out, where other people like me, who had their own versions of the BEAST would be near me. I went to Iris Place during the day, after struggling with taking a shower and getting dressed. Bed head was my only option for a hairstyle at that time, and it didn't matter what I wore. I was struggling with a great amount of weight, which enraged and bruised the fit, athletic me of the old days, the better version of myself that had at one time only fourteen percent body fat. This newer version of me looked like a beached whale, and there was no way I could get slimmer, as exercise was not possible in that state. It exceeded my capacity, and the BEAST really had a field day with my appearance. I felt terribly self-conscious, as though I would scare children away from me.

The weight gain was also due to my psychiatric medicine, and that angered me. The monster of depression ravaged me inside out to a point where I started having body dysmorphia. I felt like a freak, but I went to Iris Place anyway. Most of the time, I sat with the sweet woman who was the Education/Socialization Director. I would play a simple game like dominoes with her help. Honestly, in that state, I had trouble concentrating on the simplest of activities. I would mingle with some of the people in the educational groups, which for someone with a Master's degree in clinical psychology seemed quite mundane, so I took on the role of a junior therapist, just to fit in. Spending some quality time in these groups on a regular schedule, I gradually realized that I did not feel so alone, so isolated in my suffering. No matter what the functioning level of the clientele was, the suffering was the one common thing with which I could connect, and so I felt a little less alone. The feeling of my own suffering and pain as the most miserable phenomenon was gradually subsiding, as I found fellow sufferers.

I still wanted to die from time to time, but some part of me wanted to live more than I wanted to die, so I soldiered onward. I knew that I had to keep putting one foot in front of the other, or else the pain would get worse. I wanted my life back so badly, and I knew deep within that I had to live my life despite this pain and torment, or else I would be in a black hole, just pushing myself further toward suicide and self-destruction. This surely can be a terminal illness, eating away the body, mind and soul, bit by bit.

Chapter Six: The Beginning and Waning of Hope

Slowly, I was starting to get a little better. My depression was still at a 7.5, but I had some fleeting moments of less agony. Those brief moments gave me some hope. After a long period of struggling with therapists, I started seeing a PLAN therapist and got the name of a psychiatrist who was able to listen to me. He gave me a lot of the right kind of medicine, something no other psychiatrist had been able to do. He apparently saw through my "together" persona and actually tried to listen to the episodes of my agony that I narrated to him. Trusting him, I tried anti-psychotics, mood stabilizers, and anti-anxiety meds like clonazepam. I tried many of them, AND….they helped me with the brain pain! The medicine cocktail I was taking lessened the grip the bipolar illness had on me. WHAT A RELIEF!

Unfortunately, psychiatric medicine was not good enough to take my depression totally away, For most people, the medicines help quite a bit, but you still have to put in the hard work of finding support, finding structure, finding meaning, asking for help, getting up every day, etc. But, Paula had hope for me. I could feel her strength, her self-assurance and her true belief that I could recover. Sometimes it takes someone else to hold your hope for

you when you are blinded with pain. She offered me a
volunteer job at PLAN, answering the phones. It gave me
a reason to get up, and it was the PLAN staff, who did
not have mental illness, who filled me with hope and
sustenance. A little bit of me was starting to heal
alongside the pain.

I volunteered there for at least a year or more. It was safe,
there was structure and a routine to it that suited me best,
and it kept me moving and active, rather than staying in
my apartment ruminating and suffering. However, I was
still struggling and beginning to realize that I would have
to continue to live with some pain indefinitely. I had no
other option but to accept it as a fact, but at least it had
lessened. To this day, I desperately hope for a cure. Night
time was the worst. Being alone in an empty apartment
caused a tormenting pain in my heart. Before, I always
had family, roommates or a boyfriend that I lived with. I
did not like living alone one bit, I still don't, so I have a
roommate. I wanted to scream. I felt so alone. Not
having people to interact with or to love, and be loved by
hurt my heart. I was heartbroken. However, I endured. I
kept hoping that I could still find the right cocktail of
meds that would lessen the pain even more, so I kept
moving forward with my life.

I mentioned to Paula that I thought I could do the job as the Education/Socialization Director at Iris Place. I told her to keep me in mind, should that job ever open up in the future. A while later, Paula told me the position was becoming available, as the newest director would soon be terminated. I had a Master's Degree in Clinical Psychology, I had nearly 30 years of lived experience with acute mental illness, and I knew that I could do this, though the BEAST always asked me, "aren't you too fucked up to take that on?" And, so it came to pass. I eventually became the Education/Socialization/Director of PLAN. I had gotten off Social Security Disability, and I was employed there for eight years, until the BEAST became too much for me to work effectively and I quit. I reapplied for disability, and received it on a second attempt. Without the constraints and stress of a full time job, I then started to do well. I was exercising, spending time with friends and family, made a Wellness Recovery Action Plan (WRAP). I kept seeing my psychiatrist and therapist, and I kept going to PLAN and socializing. I was on the mend. But then I got a phone call from my sisters asking me if I would go live with my ailing parents so that I could relieve the caregiver since it was getting so expensive to have her both day and night. I didn't want to do it, but my sense of duty and my sisters' pressure kicked in and I agreed.

I couldn't predict the way an unstructured environment would affect my mental state, as I had moved into my parents' home, away from Iris Place and my friends.

One day in 2015, I woke up in the morning with excruciating mental pain. I was living with my dad who was 92 years old with deteriorating health, and my mother who was 91 suffering from the advanced stages of Alzheimer's disease. As time passed, the BEAST grew larger again as I watched my parents decline. I had been babysitting my parents at night. This would have been stressful for someone without a chronic mental illness! I slept with my mother in her king-sized bed until she became incontinent and moved to a hospital bed. I slept beside her on that king-sized bed and watched her intermittently through the night as she would try to climb over the rails on the hospital bed in her attempt to get out of it. I had to soothe her by caressing her head and slowly pulling her legs back into the bed and tuck her in. This happened usually once or twice a night. I was doing this to help my family afford Irene, the caregiver who we all thought of as family.

Another reason that the BEAST became louder, was that I was no longer working at this time, and lost my sense of structure. However, one wonderful thing happened. I noticed that when my mother's symptoms worsened to a certain point, she became nice. She became the mother I had always hoped for because she was transformed into a loving and sweet woman. It helped me to forgive her for all her misgivings with me, her history of craziness. Her disease progressed slowly and it was painful to watch her slip into a vortex as she stopped recognizing her family. She had to be fed by someone and was also in diapers. Since I was not working and had little to do during the day, and my parents lived far away from my friends, I remained isolated, as I only had Irene, to talk with during the day. My dad and I had little to talk about, and my mother was unable to communicate anyway. She was unable to complete any activities of daily living.

As I had developed cataracts during this phase, I could not drive at night to see my friends. My life felt meaningless and I was spiraling into the dark depths of my illness. Everything I was experiencing in life at this juncture, my isolation, lack of structure, lack of support from either family or friends, my parents' deteriorating health, and my anticipatory grief and depression, all of it contributed to building that perfect storm.

One fateful day, I got all of my psychotropic meds together and drove to McDonald's and bought two large water bottles/containers. I drove to a rather isolated neighborhood and parked my car there, hoping I would be discovered after I died. I did not want my family to think I was a missing person. With no fear of dying, I swallowed all my pills, quite an enormous amount of them. Surely, this would be sufficient to complete the act. I wanted to die because I could not stand the excruciating pain in my head and the torment that I was subjected to any longer. I just HAD to have the pain go away. I left a suicide note which basically said that it was nobody's fault and to please not blame yourselves. The note was never found, even though I had left it on the passenger seat in the car. It was just that the pain was so intense that I saw no hope and I felt trapped, as if I was on fire and had to extinguish it. I never thought I would have attempted suicide, but the pain was just too much for me at that time. The BEAST had narrowed my thinking, and I saw no other way out of my situation.

When I woke up in the ICU, the first images I saw were the faces of my two sisters and my brother-in-law. I remembered my family looking confused and dismayed. I remembered being enraged and miserable, finding that I was still alive! I did not know how to address the shell-shocked look on my family's faces or to answer any of their questions as the pain in my head was gone, probably from all the drugs I had taken. However, the thought of the pain coming back was horrendously scary.

I got to know when I regained my senses that someone had found me in an unconscious state in my car. The police came and broke into my car by breaking the back windshield and pulling me out. I have no idea though, why my suicide note was never found. Since I was unconscious, I do not know much about what happened, but later my sister Bonnie told me that I had tubes coming out of me everywhere, and that I looked dead. I do not remember them being angry with me, but my sister Susan told me boldly and categorically never to repeat such an act ever again. I was sent to a rehabilitation center for older patients with mental illness. When I was sent there, I came to know that most of them had Alzheimer's disease. When I got there, I asked for a clonazepam. The nurse denied me this. I was so angry that I started yelling at her.

Finally, they gave in to my cries and repeated appeals and gave me the pill. I later saw that they had written down "mixed episode" on my chart. I thought I was just depressed, but I was hugely agitated too. I wasn't just being assertive. The BEAST had come back in full force, and now I had to spend three weeks with elderly dementia patients. I sat in groups where hardly anyone could communicate. The feeling of suicide was still kicking in me, making me vulnerable all over again. How would my stay with such ailing, elderly people help me regain my mental, emotional health?

Once again, the system let me down. My roommate in the hospital tried to steal my eyeglasses on top of it all.

The psychiatrist I saw in the rehabilitation center unknowingly taught me how to kill myself, not taking it into consideration that I may still be suicidal and lying about it. He informed me quite plainly what pills would have killed me, had I taken more of them. I also lied to my outpatient psychiatrist when he asked me if I was still suicidal, so I could hoard more of those pills. After a series of tribulations, I found a new outpatient therapist to whom I told the truth about my suicidal thought, revealing that it was still an option in my mind. The prior therapist stopped taking Medicare insurance which raised the price so much that I couldn't afford her, and she said she didn't want to work with me anymore due to my suicide attempt. What horrific timing, and probably unethical, and dangerous for my vulnerable sick self. But, she did me a favor. This new therapist kept on counselling me until I felt less depressed and abandoned the plan of suicide altogether, and she worked on a sliding scale payment plan; it was free! I thought I could stick to my vow of not trying suicide no matter what, but I was wrong. Bipolar disorder can be life-threatening, and in the most agonizing moments, suicidal tendencies can overpower the brain. As I have stated over and over, the BEAST is very insidious. I found that out the hard way.

Chapter Seven: Hope Becomes Reality

I eventually had the chance to move out of my parents' house after my father died and my mother was placed in the care of doctors in a nursing home. I moved into a two-bedroom apartment with a friend. I felt safe in my new apartment and in the company of my friend now, mostly because I managed to stay stable after the death of my father. I watched him in his final moments as he passed away, and although I felt very sad to let him go, his crossing over to another world was also peaceful. My grief for my father's death did not spiral me down into a depression. During this time, I still visited my mother about once a week in the memory care unit of the nursing home. I was very sad watching her declining health and memory every time I visited her. However, I found it much easier to visit her in the nursing home than to live with her, so I was more or less happy and thankful for this arrangement.

The realities of my life and my unique living situation brought me back to North Dallas where I was closer to my friends and to Iris Place. Being here, I had much more emotional support that led to my healing. I also tried two new medications one called Vraylar, a second generation anti-psychotic and later one called Caplyta that had ultimately proven to be miraculous for me. My mornings were still difficult, but once I showered and started the day, my mood improved. Over time, my fantasies of dying subsided. I still had some fleeting suicidal ideation, but was not planning anything. Though my mental illness was still there, I was feeling safer as the symptoms of anguish, aggression and self-destruction decreased. I was also assured that my therapist told me at the end of each session to call her if I needed her before the next scheduled session. It indicated that I was no longer ignored or rejected, and thus it gave me a safety net. Other therapists whom I had seen previously would tell me to call them if I felt suicidal, and that too, was infrequent. This new therapist, on the other hand, assured me every session without fail that I could call, that she was there for me, which made a huge difference to me. Remember, the BEAST likes to isolate and can make one feel unworthy of attention.

Around this time, Iris Place turned into a Clubhouse for the mentally ill. A Clubhouse is not a place for therapy, nor is it a place to go to play cards or billiards. It is a place that has a work ordered day, and where the members (in this case those suffering from severe and persistent mental illnesses) work together to form a self-sustaining non-profit organization. There were different units that function inside the clubhouse. The culinary unit consisted of a voluntary group of members who plan menus, budget for groceries, purchase groceries, make lunch, serve lunch and clean-up after the lunch is over. Members were not paid, although paid staff assisted them. There were other units and activities, such as the clerical unit. The members of the Clubhouse would often visit museums, restaurants, and have picnics for socializing among themselves. They also celebrate holidays together on the date of the holiday, so those without family have a place to go. The Clubhouse, open five days a week from 9a.m.-4p.m, came as a blessing to me in many ways. It is called PLAN, the first accredited Clubhouse in Dallas, Texas. PLAN now stood for People Living Active Now. The environment of the Clubhouse and its various activities infused a structure and routine in my own life, quite unknowingly, thus helping me to get a bit more stable. The nature of the Clubhouse was therapeutic in itself.

With the Clubhouse being my new refuge, I have a place to go where others understand my BEAST and I understand their struggles. We all have some form of brain pain, so there is little judgment. In this safe haven, the stigma of mental illness is not present though many of the members experience self-stigma. Self-stigma is when one buys into the skewed, prejudiced, erroneous beliefs that society holds about mental illness and loses his/her self-esteem. It takes hard work to root out those social untruths, again gifted by the BEAST. However, we can learn how to weed out those thoughts with practice and with the support of good therapists. There is hope that we can bounce back and start living a meaningful life yet again.

Without the Clubhouse in my life that became my safe haven, nurtured my ravaged mind and soul, I would surely be lost. It has been a lifesaver at the time that I needed one the most. So, with better, more proper medication, a great therapist, a stable living condition (I live near the Clubhouse), and a good support system, I am pleased to say I have been relatively stable for these last few years. I still have my morning depression, but I can manage it much better than I used to earlier. . In addition, I was asked to become a certified mental health peer specialist by the director of the PLAN Clubhouse. Just like Paula had faith in me, so did Ruth. I received a scholarship and took a 40 hour certificate course where I learned how to use my lived experience with mental health issues to help others who are mentally ill. I also learned how to tell my "story" in hopes of inspiring others to do the same. We also had to complete 250 hours of working with peers, and have supervision before we could get our certificate. I now have a part time job working with people with severe mental illness and use my lived experience to guide them and assist them. I have been doing it for over 2 years. So, I can say that life has come full circle from the days of psychosis, depression, mania, and misery. I have a purpose and my pain that I suffered for so long is not going to waste as I learned a lot of lessons from it.

When Covid-19 pandemic hit, life at the Clubhouse was impacted too, just like any other center or institution. When we were forced to shelter in place, the Clubhouse organized a conference call at 1.15 p.m. every Monday through Friday and around 25 members called to check in and share how they were feeling, and it helped a lot to alleviate the tremendous isolation that we all were feeling in such a situation. It was a support system that worked well. We still worked at the Clubhouse by doing meaningful tasks such as submitting articles for our newsletter by e-mail. The Clubhouse has a Facebook page. I managed to run a 6 p.m. support call. Other phone in activities led by members occurred at 3 pm, Monday through Friday. The structure and routine which was part of our lives throughout Covid-19, has formed the essence of my persona now, and though the pandemic had taken a toll on our social lives for some time, I managed to sail through, like the others.

The Covid-19 pandemic was an isolating time for most people. The enemy of mental illness, however, is isolation, for it leads to rumination on negative thoughts and that leads to suffering. When we are in pain our inclination is to pull away from others and rest. Unfortunately, to recover from mental illness we have to have others around us, to help us think well. We need therapists, psychiatrists, understanding friends, emotional support, community, and structure. It takes a village, and it takes fortitude to get up and get going when you are in emotional pain. However, to beat the BEAST you have to dig deep. With mental illness the saying "no pain no gain" is accurate, and I am so sorry it is like that. The good news is that the medicines are getting better, as research into mental illness is allowing for more understanding of the genes and mechanisms that are faulty and cause such brain pain. BE BRAVE, BE RESILIENT, AND BE OPEN MINDED TO CHANGE. DO NOT GIVE UP, DO NOT ISOLATE, FIGHT FOR YOUR LIFE, FIND STRUCTURE, AND KNOW YOU CAN FIND PEACE OF MIND. But most importantly REACH OUT FOR HELP! Help exists now more than ever.

Please seek help from trained professionals if my symptoms seemed to resonate with you. They have much better medicine now and are also better equipped to treat patients with various forms of mental illness than they did in the 1970's, when I myself was misdiagnosed. They now know that antidepressants can cause mania if one is misdiagnosed with MDD when the underlying disease is bipolar disorder. They also have a variety of mood stabilizers that help people suffering from bipolar disorder, and they have antipsychotics which help with anxiety as well as psychosis. New medications are coming on the market more readily. There is a lot to be hopeful for. The therapists today have more accurate understanding of the illness, there are peer-led support groups, there are Mental Health Peer Specialists, and there are mental health Clubhouses where others with the same or similar diagnoses hang out. The Clubhouse model is especially beneficial once you come out of an episode of hospitalization for your illness. It provides structure and understanding by its members when you are still feeling vulnerable.

I wish you luck on your journey towards wellness. Remember, it takes a village to get well, so embrace your inner fortitude and realize you are stronger than you think you are so never give up the fight to live a stable and productive life. You've Got This!

Family celebrating my new car and new found independence

"There came a time when the risk to remain tight in the bud was more painful than the risk it took to blossom"

Anais Nin

PART II: THE OTHER SIDE OF THE COUCH

I would now like to pass on some of the wisdom and insights I have gathered from my many years of being mentally ill and working extensively with people with SMI. I cover over 20 valuable suggestions that might be useful in identifying aspects of your mental illness while you are in recovery. Recovery doesn't mean getting back to where you were before the BEAST got you, or never having symptoms again. It is a journey of learning how to live alongside your mental illness and still have a meaningful and productive life. Feel free to read them in any order and I hope that they are helpful.

Chapter Eight: Understanding the BEAST from My Perspective

Anhedonia - A hedonist is a person who seeks pleasure, hence, anhedonia means lack of pleasure. In depression, the lack of feeling pleasure is a painful reality. The world outside may be fantastic, one may have received a raise at work, one may have won the lottery, but one cannot feel the pleasure of those fortunate happenings. One cannot feel pleasure across the board; NOTHING is pleasurable. It is a horrible feeling. Anhedonia is cruel. Even when I explain it to people, sometimes when something good happens to me, they ask me, "doesn't this make you feel better?" And I have to say, "No, it does not, simply because I cannot feel pleasure when anhedonia is in my experience." I often fake feeling happy to survive in this world. And, I do not always have anhedonia with my illness, so I can feel pleasure at times. But anhedonia is the BEAST'S lethal weapon. Imagine not being able to feel pleasure for days, months, years and even decades! You would be miserable too. Sometimes your meds could be the reason for your anhedonia, so talk to your psychiatrist about it. Just know you are not alone in your anhedonia; it is a struggle. Keep putting one foot in front of the other when you have it. After all, the effort of continuing to move on with your life helps fight the BEAST.

Assertiveness - I once thought quite mistakenly that being assertive was about standing up for yourself until you got what you wanted. So, under the guise of assertiveness I would throw tantrums in an attempt to get someone to give me what I wanted. True assertiveness is about standing up for yourself with a calm manner, and being respectful of the other person's thoughts and feelings. When we have a need and we don't act assertively in the situation, we have to push it into the unconscious, and our anger, when turned inward, can cause depression, or even intensify our existing depression. There is a difference between aggressiveness and assertiveness. When we are assertive, we feel like a respectful and thoughtful person with self-esteem. However, when we are aggressive, we turn into bullies and do not feel very good about ourselves for acting so harshly. So, it is important to study assertiveness and practice it. It helps calm the BEAST in the long run.

Anosognosia - This is a medical condition when a sick person doesn't know they are ill. It is different from denial, which is a psychological phenomenon. Anosognosia happens when the brain, mainly the frontal lobe, has lesions, or during a psychotic illness, whereby one cannot know they are ill because of the disruption to the neurotransmitters in the frontal lobe. Therefore, it is possible for someone with bipolar disorder to not know they are sick. There is a wonderful book about this called, I'm not sick, I don't need help, by Xavier Amador. The book is listed in the bibliography section of this book, and should be read by everyone affected by mental illness. The book has instructions on how to work with someone who has this condition.

So, one can be manic and not have a clue they are ill. Hence, they often don't take their medication and their illness worsens. It is very difficult for the families of one suffering from anosognosia as they watch their loved one deteriorate. A person suffering from this malady can end up in jail, homeless, or even dead. Anosognosia is very dangerous. It would be very wise to read up on it, for it could save lives, or at least a lot of needless suffering.

Coping With Suicidal Thoughts – It has been observed that when one has major depressive episodes, they often will have suicidal thoughts. The torment and pain of depression makes one feel helpless. When the pain gets severe or long lasting enough, suicidal thoughts will enter one's mind. Suicide is the ultimate form of fantasy to escape from the pain. It is a response to the BEAST. In my experience, I never really wanted to die and leave the world and my near and dear ones when I was feeling suicidal, I just wanted the torment, the excruciating pain to stop. However, we must learn to cope with suicidal ideation. We have to understand that the pain is narrowing our ability to cope, and that the BEAST is telling us that the torment within us will never end. For many, the pain has in fact been a long road and the hopelessness has snowballed. We have all heard about "learned helplessness", a conditioned response that makes people feel like there is no option that is sufficient enough to change a situation; therefore, the person becomes helpless. In my own experience, depression contains both "learned helplessness" and "learned hopelessness". It is a downward slope, leading to suicide. I sincerely believe those who attempt suicide or complete suicide do so mainly because of the helplessness and hopelessness of not seeing a way out of the intense pain.

So, we go to other people in search of finding hope. We narrate our misery to our therapists, family, and friends. What we are looking for is hope because we cannot find it within. The pain is too blinding, the BEAST too big for us to conquer, or so it feels. But we can cope with the BEAST once we realize what we have been doing. We can create a team of people who can think well for us when our thoughts are obstructed in our anguished state. We can learn to tell people when we have lost our hope. We can tell them what we need to hear, and not just wish for it. We often hope and wish miracles will occur. We can learn how to communicate without aggravating people or being aggravated in return. When we convey to someone that we feel suicidal, we alarm them. However, there are better ways to communicate our despair. Telling them that we feel unbearable pain and that we don't know how to cope is more helpful. We can learn to take them in confidence and ask for their help in that way, so that they are not intimidated and frightened by our presence. Although the BEAST can narrow our thinking to the point of suicide, we can commit to ourselves to learn how to cope with suicidal thoughts and feelings with a much more positive approach. We can make a conscious decision that we will not harm ourselves, that we will tell someone of our thoughts, and remember that "this too shall pass," even when our brain might be pulling us in the other direction. To know the BEAST is to beat him.

It means taking responsibility for our recovery, which means moving forward when we are in pain, rather than just pulling up the covers and letting the BEAST have its way with us. So, you say, "I don't have family or a 'team' to help me." You can make one, as I did. I changed one psychiatrist after another until I found one that heard my outpourings and helped me in a constructive way. You can do the same. I did the same with therapists. I moved on to different people until I found the best one for me, one that not only heard me, but was also responsive to the BEAST. One who had hope for me when I was blindsided. Slowly, gradually, I have found friends in support groups, while I learned how to ask my family and friends for what I need in a better way. You too can do all of that and more. It's up to you. If your BEAST tells you that you can't do it, find the hero within yourself to prove the BEAST wrong. Fight for your recovery, for that is what it takes. Too many people commit suicide before they have had a chance to fight back. You can. Let people know of your hopelessness and feelings of helplessness early so you can survive in spite of the excruciating struggles and chaos reigning within you. It's the only way. Don't be isolated in this battle for your survival.

Do Distorted Thoughts Really Cause Depression? - So much of the literature in the studies of human psychology tells us that our thoughts cause our feelings and that distorted thinking can cause depression. Therefore, practitioners use Cognitive Therapy to try to alleviate depression. Change your thoughts and you would not feel worthless, or ugly, or whatever the BEAST makes you feel you are. From my experience with a depressive disorder, it is the reverse. It is the brain dysfunction that causes the negative thinking and a depressed brain gets stuck in the quagmire of pain like an engine in first gear. Most of the times, it cannot get out of first gear where one can think logically. So, the depressed brain ruminates over and over in a loop, unable to see the simple answer. For example, when I am deeply depressed, everything takes enormous energy and seems like a big deal to me. I cannot process it. I don't know what's going on in my brain in those moments, it feels like I cannot use my prefrontal cortex to sort things out. I can't switch gears or stop ruminating. I have cognitive distortions that stick to my being like glue.

Cognitive distortions, on the other hand, happen when one misattributes things. For example, "Catastrophizing" is when one thinks the outcome will only come out negative. Cognitive Therapy was created to help one to change or alter the course of these thoughts and think of a more balanced view of things. When I am in a deep depression, no amount of positive or accurate thinking helps much. It makes me feel like a failure. I don't think working on correcting cognitive distortions is harmful when one is only mildly depressed. In fact, it is helpful. For severe depression, medicine makes the largest difference, followed by perseverance, and time. Once you have found a medicine that alleviates the pain to a large degree, then work on your cognitive distortions.

I have experienced this for myself, and witnessed in others a large degree of frustration from professionals who harp on cognitive distortions in people who are already in enormous distress, and cannot get out of first gear. In most psychiatric hospitals, you even have to go to classes and be inundated with lessons on how to change your thinking, which is very likely to make you feel worse. The time is just not right for all that education. Repeatedly attempted, these education techniques may do more harm than good, filling you up with depression instead of hope. With major depression, the BEAST has a grip of its own. If we could think positive, we would be doing so, and not be in this predicament to begin with. Think if it were any physical ailment, what would that person do? Would one ask a person having a gall bladder attack to think positive or alternate thoughts? Our brains are not working correctly, yet, this is what often is offered to us. There is so much we do not know yet about the brain and its mysteries.

So, forgive people who push it on you when they do not understand how hard you have already tried so many of those techniques. A better way when the BEAST is ruminating on all of your failures, is to try to distract it from those thoughts. Try to catch yourself when you are ruminating and take an action, however small, to get your brain to move away from the negative loop. If you find it hard to concentrate, try small steps such as playing a game on your computer, or calling someone and ask them to talk about something distracting, or take a medicine that has been prescribed by your psychiatrist for those moments. The less you indulge the BEAST, the more peace of mind you might find around yourself. This is not easy to accomplish, but will surely be of help.

When you feel well, think about your little and big milestones in life, your successes and accomplishments. It can help you to focus on what you have done well and your attributes. Ask others who love you to write down what it is they love about you, and let yourself feel it too. Take it all in! Read it over and over. When you are depressed, the BEAST will find ways to make you feel like they were lying. Never forget, the BEAST is a liar.

Life Consists of Many and Varied Feelings - Not everything can be categorized or defined as depression.

When we get depressed, it is easy not to recognize what we are feeling because we are in so much pain; therefore, many ordinary transient feelings stress our already exhausted brain and cause symptoms of depression. With increased stressors, it is possible for us to become overwhelmed or even suicidal. In my experience, it has been important to do my best to recognize the feelings of the moment when I am experiencing them, so that I do not just throw every one into the depression basket. When we ignore our feelings of anger, frustration, insecurity, those emotions get repressed and eventually make us more symptomatic. The challenge is in recognizing what we are feeling and how we are going to deal with it. For example, if someone says something to me that makes me feel angry, I have to acknowledge to myself that I am feeling angry. Then, I have to decide what to do with my anger: Should I say something? Or should I just be aware of it and keep it to myself? The worst alternative is to not recognize it and let it go into the sub-conscious layer of your mind only to become symptomatic with depression a day later and not know why. However, when I keep in touch with my feelings, acknowledge them, I am one step ahead of the game. It is hard work, but it pays large dividends.

People who haven't experienced a chronic brain illness such as depression often do not understand why people with brain illnesses need to go to psychotherapy year after year. Psychotherapy makes one aware of his/her feelings and makes him/her learn how to effectively deal with them. In addition, they may need help in problem solving, dealing with shame, forgiveness, and helplessness to name but a few. Life is difficult, especially when your brain, your motor, is not working correctly. I often say I am functioning on one and a half cylinders because that is how it feels. Our brains are busy working hard to fight the BEAST, not just the problems of daily living.

So, know that you have double duty. You have to pay attention to the BEAST and also to the outer world. Try processing your feelings as they arise, or take the time at the end of the day to revisit what happened during the course of that day and see if you can put to rest some of the struggles of that day. If you turn a blind eye to this, the BEAST will have a field day, and you might not be able to function for long periods. Do not let the hard work deter you; it is worth it.

Suffering - No one on earth likes to suffer. However, if you have clinical depression, the fact is, you will suffer.

It is an acute and often chronic brain illness, and you have done nothing to deserve this suffering. Life is difficult enough without the added burden of depression. And we deserve to moan about it. But, at some point, we must put aside our moaning and put on our boxing gloves and fight it intelligently. Anger can get in the way of this. I know; I have had my share. I still have my moments of fury over my fate. I have learned to catch myself when I am moaning about the unfairness of it all and also learned to turn to problem solving. I have also learned on the way that we can live life alongside our suffering. I have mostly been employed full time, except for some years on disability. What I gained from that was a sense of meaning and purpose. When I look back on the things I've done, I don't remember the pain. I remember what I did for love and the people I met and loved by putting one foot in front of the other. Despite the pain that we are subjected to, we must remember to endure and survive with courage and dignity, for it's the best way to soften the BEAST, to let him know he cannot have all of us. He takes enough.

I have also had romantic relationships over the years. Though I am single now, I did not let the BEAST stop me from loving or from being loved. The BEAST loves to tell you that you are unlovable, but that is just another lie.

Do not let your suffering confuse you into thinking that no one will love you. The burden is yours, not someone else's, if you take responsibility for it. Others do find you lovable. You are not a burden; you have a burden.

Even in the midst of your suffering, medication and treatments hold the promise of relief, though some side effects may be burdensome. I have tried over 20 medications and still tweak my medicines even now. Some were harmless, but did not work to reduce my suffering. Others had horrible side effects that seemed worse than the illness itself. By suffering wisely in the face of discomfort and agony, and persevering, I eventually came up with a more effective combination of drugs, keeping me as stable as I could be. Once new medications and treatments become available, I will try some of those as well. I am determined to manage my symptoms until science has a better handle about what has gone wrong with my brain and how to fix it. But, until that day, I will try to use the knowledge and insights I have gained from my suffering to push forward in my recovery.

There are many lessons in suffering if we can just open up to them. For example, I am much more sensitive and aware of other people's sufferings which makes me more understanding and compassionate towards my fellow humans. I know that even though we can't always see suffering in others, it is there in ways that make them respond to their capacity. We can also use our knowledge of suffering to reach out and help others, giving more perspective to our ordeal. We can pass on our knowledge and save others from going down the wrong path by sharing our experiences so they can divert from needless suffering. We can find the strength in ourselves that we did not know existed in the first place. In short, we can grow dramatically toward the good if we suffer with wisdom and dignity.

Chapter Nine: Understanding the Effects of the Illness

Grief - When we experience a loss, we experience grief. During the years of my immense struggle with depression, the loss of my good health, my peace of mind, was replaced with enormous grief. It is very hard to accept losing our good health to a brain illness. I cannot trust my brain. It often gives me great pain. My peace of mind leaves me and the BEAST takes over. It is like walking along and suddenly, with no warning, the ground crumbles beneath your feet, and you are in a large pit covered in debris. And, you do not know when you will get on firmer ground again. When your brain seems to have collapsed, you earnestly pray for a sense of equilibrium to return to your life. You are overwhelmed by grief and loss at various phases of your life when equilibrium doesn't return in your life. So, grief is not a static state, but an ongoing process. Again, we are summoned to cope. Naming the process is the first step to coping with it. And, it is never pleasant, but it passes if we let it.

I agree with the famous Dr. Elizabeth Kubler Ross's stages of grief. First comes shock-the feeling of disbelief when the disease happens to us, then denial-we repress the fact that this is happening. This is followed by depression- despair over our fate, then anger- rage at our fate, then bargaining-asking for a cure, and eventually acceptance- knowing and realizing we will have to live our lives by bearing this fate.

I have found that I continually experience those stages, not in any particular order, but continually in spurts. Sometimes I still wake up and am in shock that I have this brain pain. After 41 years, one would think that would pass, but it pops up often. I am in frequent denial, and think I should be able to function like any other normal person, but that is not fair to me. The BEAST does in fact very much exist, and I have not been able to go back to those easy days of waking up and feeling clear headed. Gosh, I miss those days. They were not perfect, but the burden of the BEAST is a loss for me. When I realize that I cannot go back to my pre-BEAST days, I get depressed and then the depression turns into rage, furious anger. I have learned to recognize this as grief and let it run its course. And, I have done my share of bargaining. I used to ask God if I could trade my legs for my brain to stop hurting. I could have endured better if it were my legs. But the bargaining never worked and I was left with a decision. I could rage, rage, rage against the loss of my good health, or I could accept it. At times I just let it be and accepted it, at other times I have wallowed in self-pity, and on many occasions I have raged. The trick is to know that this is all a normal emotional reaction to a very serious loss. It is normal, even though it doesn't feel so great. Knowing that grief will rear its ugly head from time to time can tame it to some degree. Recognizing the stages of grief takes some of its power away. Find safe people to vent to, do some journaling activities, do some exercise, or do what works for you to let out the feelings, and mostly know that you are not crazy. You have had a major loss that affects your life profoundly.

Grief often hits when you least expect it. Once you hear of good news or milestones made by others without brain illness, it rekindles your grief. You think then, that you might have experienced a similar joy, had the pain and the monster of depression not found you. Grief's favorite question is "Why me"? And you find no sufficient answers. That is when you have to befriend grief or at least honor it. Lost opportunities are painful. And, we deserve to moan about it. We cannot, however, get stuck in it, for we have lost enough time to the menace of suffering. Ride the wave of grief and be brave, for if you ride it long enough, it will pass. Do not hold onto it one minute longer than you have to. And, do not do it alone, use your team, the ones you confide in the most.

Anxiety and Panic Attacks - A huge dose of anxiety and panic attacks accompanied my bipolar disorder. These two best friends of the BEAST have made life hard for me in ways that I am not sure words will translate. I get a sense of not being in my body and that my voice is coming from outside of my head when I am talking. Deep within, I feel a huge sense of dread and foreboding that feels terrifying to say the least. It is the fight or flight response of my nervous system, a protective mechanism gone haywire in my brain which fires when there is no real danger. Moreover, I have fear of that 'fear' which can be paralyzing to the brain. I have tried many techniques to prevent this from happening, and the best thing that works for me is medication, and exposure to the thing that makes me anxious. I had to learn to live with this daily cycle of panic, fear, more panic, and more fear. It was a waking nightmare. If you have had a panic attack you will know what I am talking about. If you have not experienced this, then you are lucky. I envy you. To know life without the panic would be a Godsend along with relief from the BEAST. In fact, this is part of the BEAST for me. Our BEASTS all differ. So, since this is part of the BEAST for me, I have included it in this book.

I just know the burden of it has brought me to my knees in prayer many times.

You probably could not tell when I was having a panic attack because I have learned to hide them to function in life, which is also mentioned extensively in my memoir. I try to appear quiet while this particular BEAST is in full force. Your panic attacks may have more physical symptoms such as rapid heartbeat, and sweating. Those of us who "hide" our panic attacks deserve an Oscar nomination for our performance. With my new medication I have them much less often, by God's grace. And, my perseverance and exposure paid off.

Isolation- When we are in pain, we usually tend to pull into our shells and isolate. There are many reasons the BEAST causes us to want to isolate, and we have to identify them. One reason for isolation is of course, just the pain of it all. The pain can manifest itself into various other symptoms that can free us if we can only identify them. For example, rumination on negative thoughts is one reason we isolate. Rumination on negative thoughts which can make us feel worthless, stupid, fat and ugly keeps us from others. Rumination can become a bad habit, even though it is an integral part of our illness. Those negative distortions caused by the ruminations get lots of our attention and we reinforce them by letting them take over, rather than distracting ourselves from them. Sometimes the BEAST will not let us distract, or so it feels, depending upon our level of depression. At other times we need to identify rumination for what it is and get actively away from it by taking an action that distracts us. Getting up out of the house and with people will often prevent ruminating, but we generally do not do that. If we can say to ourselves "I am ruminating and I need to not isolate" we are headed in the right direction. To do this we must enlist our intestinal fortitude, for everything inside of us wants to let the rumination rule, and we must be strong and use our gut strength to stop it in its tracks.

Identifying rumination and distracting oneself from it may not work the first time, but I promise you it will work if you practice it. The hard part is moving away from it, for the ruminating BEAST is powerful, but you can be more powerful than it. You can also use distraction to help quiet anxiety when it rears its ugly head. Anxiety is depression's best friend, and these same distraction techniques can help quiet anxiety as necessary.

Another reason we isolate is learned helplessness. As mentioned earlier, learned helplessness is when there is a solution to your problem, but you have been conditioned by your past experiences to believe it will not matter what you do. Therefore, you feel no reason to change your situation, for you firmly believe you will have a negative result. So, you stop trying. For example, if you have been fired from several jobs in the past, you may give up on trying to get a job, for you firmly believe you cannot get a job. The "not trying" is learned helplessness. And individuals struggling with the BEAST often feel that they cannot attain what they are looking for, for the BEAST, in the past, stuck to them like Velcro, and trying to move forward seemed like a foolish effort. So, we must identify areas where we have learned helplessness, and look forward to the future, not backwards. We need to keep trying. Persistence most often pays dividends.

Fear is another reason we isolate. Fear of getting more depressed, of being rejected, of being found out can have horrible repercussions. The fear list is endless. We must jump back on the horse we fell off of and find our courage to face the world. Isolation leads to more pain and continuous suffering, and we surely do not need that. Remember, the BEAST loves idleness. After a while we isolate out of habit and stop realizing we are even isolating; we just feel more depressed. So, we need to be proactive and first identify that we are isolating, figure out the reason, and jump back on the horse we so fear. Just making the effort alone is valuable.

The Tendency Heading Towards Suicide -The road leading to suicide is a slippery slope. The desire to commit suicide for me has taken different forms as my illness progressed and as my coping skills increased. For a long time, I would have suicidal thoughts because I was angry. I was angry at the BEAST for my plight and also angry at others for not being able to comprehend my plight and act empathetically. The world keeps going even though one is distressed with despair beyond despair. Sometimes, if I am honest, I wanted to commit suicide just to get back at people for not understanding, or not showing any signs of understanding my suffering. They may have dismissed my feelings or I perceived some sort of real or imagined slight. So, it is wise to note your impulsive proclivities in order that you may be aware of them so you do not do something that is irreversible. Suicide is the end of your life as you know it, period.

Contemplating suicide is as excruciatingly lonely, painful act, especially if it is not just an escape fantasy, but something you really are considering. That happened to me once, other than my very real suicide attempt. I started to feel detached from this world, unconnected in a way I had never felt before. I knew I was on a slippery slope downhill, so I told my therapist about it. The thing that helped me not attempt an overdose with my prescribed medications was the reality of attempting. What if I failed to take my own life? I could end up being a vegetable with an unsuccessful attempt, I could hurt my organs and live, and just be in worse shape. Not to mention all of the people I would traumatize by acting on such a course. Those closest to me would be scarred from it, forever wondering what they could/should have done to save me. So, I decided I had to build a suicide team to prevent my disastrous actions because this was getting too big for me to handle alone. I started telling people what I was going through and asked for their support. I am still working on figuring out what I need from various people and how they can help me when I am spiraling downward. I cannot do this alone, so I rely on my team. Those of us with chronic depression need to do this to stay safe and alive. I am working on this as I write, simply because I am scared, for this illness is insidious.

To sum it all up, Suicide is a permanent outcome to a temporary problem, and a very damaging one. Depression waxes and wanes. I will keep fighting my depression, my agony, with the demons of my own mind or brain, hopefully in an efficient manner. And so will you, please. We draw our inspiration through one another. I need to see your courage if I am to access mine. Though we feel alone, in the long run, we are not.

The Hospital - Today, as I write this, I am suffering and would like to go to the hospital. My brain pain has been severe over the past month, as extreme stressors have pressed on my brain. I am in crisis, but I won't go to the hospital because I fear I will not get treated in the manner I would like. Being in a psychiatric unit is just not a helpful thing for me. What I feel I need is to be on a non-psychiatric unit, whereby my brain pain would be taken as seriously as I experience it, and I could get the rest I need. For example, on a — non-psychiatric unit, I could sleep in the morning and have breakfast brought to me. I am dead tired right now and in immense pain. On the psychiatric unit I would have to get up early and go to breakfast or miss it entirely. I could not get up in time to eat with the rest of the unit, for my brain is not functioning correctly and I am sick, just as sick as if I had appendicitis or any other physical ailment. Yet, I am expected to get up and get myself to breakfast. It's not fair. This brain pain or so-called mental illness is not about gathering myself up by the bootstraps, or a character problem. It is about real intense suffering. I need help getting fed in the morning. If I was capable of functioning well, I would not need the hospital.

Next, I would be expected to go to a meeting in the morning and perhaps even play a group game, such as tossing a balloon around. No one with pancreatitis is asked to do this, why then would we be expected to do it while having brain pain? I would also be asked to go to meetings all day long to learn about mental illness. Do diabetics go to meetings all day to learn about their disease and how to cope with it when they are in crisis? Are they asked to hang out with one another and play games together? I think not. Now, I don't mean to say there is no facility or infrastructure for rehabilitation for individuals with brain pain. However, I just want to explain that when one is in crisis, it is not the time to initiate learning. It is time for rest, for recuperation, time for the doctors to evaluate what is needed to get the person out of crisis. If I myself am in crisis, I want a call button, and get a nurse to help me to the bathroom or to give me a prn (a medication prescribed to take as needed). I also want my own television and my own telephone, basic facilities that I would get if I were in a regular hospital room. And, don't forget, I would also demand a remote control that controls my bed, my lights in the room, and calls the nursing station.

I don't want to learn about how my thoughts influence my feelings and that I should just think better thoughts. I don't want to hang around with people who have a variety of psychiatric problems and communicate with them, especially in my crisis situation. I want rest, and care, help, and analysis of my problems by trained personnel. I want to be treated like others are when they go to the hospital for their physical ailments. I do not want to take a crash course in psychological theory. Why? Because it doesn't work. I have a medical problem, a biological medical problem. One that we do not know all that much about. And, I do not want to be blamed for it. I want to be treated with dignity. I am a patient and I want to be treated like one. I am not a consumer or a client, I am a patient who needs medical attention, for my pain stems from my brain.

Traumatic Stress - If you have ever had a major depressive disorder for any length of time, you are bound to be traumatized. The pain is so vastly different from any other pain that you have had, and is out of the ordinary of every day experience in a horrible way. I can understand that you could not escape from the pain of it for quite some time. Even if antidepressants work, they can take up to six weeks before you will have symptom relief. That is enough time for the BEAST to haunt you.

If you manage to get well from it temporarily, you might still fear its return, making you hyper vigilant to any symptom ever so slightly similar to the experience of it. That is post-traumatic stress disorder, which is again a very haunting, harrowing experience in terms of one's mental, psychological health. If medication is proven to be insufficient to manage your illness, you will have continual pain. You might feel trapped in such a situation, and that is what I mean when I refer to it as traumatic stress. It is my own term, specifically for those with serious and persistent mental illness. Chronic pain that is psychic in nature is very scary. When there is little to no escape from the pain, you may develop 'learned helplessness'.

When you have learned helplessness it is hard to see options, much less act on them, when you are suffering. This can lead to learned hopelessness, eventually leading to suicide. So, we must think about digging deep if the medicines do not give enough relief from the BEAST. And we might want to keep trying new medicines prescribed by a psychiatrist. We should think about tapping into our life instinct and fight for all we are worth.

I have found hope in letting the pain just be. Let it be. If we fight too hard against the BEAST there is less wiggle room for the BEAST- free times. I have learned that I am not in charge of the universe and also maybe I was called to suffer for reasons I cannot yet understand. As I keep maturing, these reasons are becoming a little more tangible to me, as I fight to make and find meaning in all of this. The BEAST has challenged me in ways I cannot even explain, nor did I ever think I could endure, but I did endure them, and still do. You can too. Do not collapse when the stress of this trauma gets to you; grieve if you must, but keep on fighting the good fight. Look at this as a challenge instead of a burden, even though it is burdensome.

Your attitude is important in your fight. Find the underlying optimist in yourself. If you are still alive, you still have it in you. Even if you may have post-traumatic stress or traumatic stress, you must believe that today is a new day, a new chance to find your hope and fight back.

Back To The Hospital - Since I began this book, I had a two-month psychiatric hospitalization. I was very sick and suicidal, transitioning from a medicine I was taking to feeling good to crashing. I was experiencing the most severe pain that I can ever remember, and I saw only a slim glance at getting better. It was the same week Robin Williams committed suicide. I tried many medicine trials, only to feel worse. Then Electro Convulsive Shock Therapy (ECT) treatment was introduced. I watched a video about people who were not functioning due to depression and how ECT somehow revived their spirits and their mental health. I was nervous about having it done, but I felt I had no other choice. I went for eight sessions. At about the fourth session my rigid suicidal thought process lessened a whole lot. But again, I had a bad reaction during my eighth session. I went into some kind of fugue state, a temporary state of confusion whereby I couldn't tell if I was dreaming or if things were real. It was tremendously scary. I also could not tell when people were talking to me. I was so spaced out.

Fortunately, that went away; I was fearful that I would not be able to go back to normal, but I did. I also heard music in my head for about two months after the ECT. It was a symphony of songs I knew that played in my head round the clock, constantly repeating themselves. I refused any further ECT treatment; therefore, I did not get an entire regimen. It takes courage and desperation to allow people to shock your brain! But, those first four sessions probably stopped me from attempting suicide. I would encourage people who are severely depressed and find that nothing is working for them to be open-minded about it. It works like a miracle for some people. There are risks involved in undergoing this journey, though, including the strange side effects which I experienced. However, ECT is not like putting on a band aid. You go under anesthesia, have multiple sessions and it is not without risk.

And then there were the hospital groups, and I have already mentioned previously that I disliked those groups. I did find out one thing that was helpful about all the group classes that I had the choice to attend. The structure of the classes helped me get well. I do not know if we need psychiatric classes, but we do need a reason to get out of bed, despite how hard that can be. The truth is that pulling the sheets up over your head will not effectively put your illness into remission. It is hard to get out of a depression, even with the best of medication. So, it seems that structure is the best ingredient. So, go out there and find structure.

Volunteer, find something meaningful to get you out of bed in the morning. I grew up with the slogan, "JUST DO IT" even when it is hard.

Battle Fatigue - Living with a chronic mental illness comes with battle fatigue. Every morning I have a battle with myself about getting up and functioning. I do not want to face the pain my illness gives me. The simplest act of getting out of bed and taking a shower to start the day seems to be the hardest decision. Morning is a depressing time for me. Just like a combat veteran who doesn't want to deal with going into combat, I too, do not want to face the BEAST. I haven't seen much about this condition being described or explained in the literature on depression. I am tired of the fear, the fear of having to go through the day, not knowing what pain will come. It's like walking in a mine field.

I have various levels of experience while coping with this condition. I usually have to visualize a nice warm shower for a long time and how much better I will feel when I am clean. Sometimes this works and gets me into the shower. Other times I use fear to motivate myself, the fear that I will lose a job or my mind and be without money and structure whatsoever in my daily life if I don't get up and get going. I am not talking about the typical feeling of detesting to get out of bed in the morning, I know that feeling well, for I have had my share of it before I got sick. This is downright paralyzing fear. I would rather stay in my bed with the warm covers and the safety of little to no stress than to get up. But, my life instinct pushes me forward. I fear staying sick or getting sicker more than I fear getting up and facing my illness. I think I am lucky that way, but I would rather get out of bed due to a great desire to enjoy the day like I used to, before the BEAST found me. However, it is what it is, and it is with the hope that one day I will have that great desire to get up again if a cure is found for this depressive illness I have. My brain is tired and exhausted. Having a brain illness is like undertaking a marathon, except you do not have a fit body in the end, you just have another day to face.

I remember when I was really ill with my brain illness, I could not work at a vocation. So, I went to a local Starbucks every morning just as if I were going to work. I met some wonderful people, and over time they would call me if I had not yet arrived. We had coffee together, but more importantly, we had developed a sense of community. And, in coming to care about one another, we had a shared bond, and some meaning in our lives. It kept me alive at the time. And I would probably do this again if I would lose a job in the future. We should try to fight our battle fatigue with something more powerful than our own will, and that is often found in connecting with others. A committed friend will do the trick too, and we cannot diminish our importance for that friend, no matter what the BEAST tells us. We must imprint that on our souls so we can get up each day with fortitude and determination, no matter how difficult or how horrible, or terrified we feel. If we uphold this thought firmly, with utmost positivity, we can get up and take that shower. Maybe not every day, but most days.

Jealousy - I am jealous of people who do not have a brain illness. Not all people and also not all the time, but at times when I am experiencing brain pain, I think that everyone has it so much easier than I do in my own life. During those moments, I want to scream and let out all my agony. Of course, they have their own respective struggles, but they have the luxury of being able to trust that the BEAST will not come and take them out of the game. I do not know if I will be able to experience long periods of brain stability ever in this lifetime. Frankly, it makes me furious. When the BEAST hits me hard, I think that every other person has more to offer to the world than I do, or at least experience a lot more happiness. And it fries my back side. "Nuff" said.

Shame - Shame is at the BEAST'S core. It is the feeling of worthlessness at the core that the BEAST doles out, which makes it all the more painful. And, there are many stigmatizing messages that the BEAST offers to us. This feeling of shame is quite different from feeling ashamed of a behavior that falls short of the mark. Shame doesn't want to let you off the hook, while being ashamed is simply a form of sin that can be pardoned once one has admitted contrition. Hence, shame is entirely a personal feeling, and being ashamed is more about uncomfortable behavior.

From my own experience, I can share that when I am sick, the BEAST tells me in many ways that I have character flaws and that if I would just pull myself up by the boot straps, I could snap out of it. During those moments, I feel shame. A large part of society feels the same way. Even though I know that the stigma regarding brain illness is spread through the undereducated, I still buy into some of that. And, the BEAST is never happier that I do.

It also feels like I cannot at times separate myself from my Illness, due to the workings of my brain. And, I feel shame. I start in with the "should haves" and "should not haves." I tell myself I should be able to do this or that thing even though I am running on one cylinder. Or, I tell myself I should not be feeling this way that I am terribly overreacting when I am depressed. So how does one start to begin working on their shame-filled thoughts? There are things one can do.

First, we must get educated on our illness. We should attempt to learn as much we can about the particular brain illness we have. Knowledge is power. If I know that my neurotransmission system is out of order, which is causing me symptoms, I can remind myself of that. I can also ask others to remind me of that. I believe we also have to come to a large degree of acceptance of the fact that our brains will act uncontrollably at times and those are the times when we will have symptoms. When I am symptom free, I still think sometimes that I am cured and it will never happen again. When it does, I feel paralyzed. We have to accept, just like in any chronic illness, that symptoms will come. It doesn't mean defeat, and we must do our best to bounce back from our illness. We must also fight back against our desire to believe our feelings. Sometimes what we feel has nothing to do with what is reality, and most importantly, our depressive feelings are often not reliable. For example, when we feel worthless, that is inherently untrue, yet it feels true.

We must always remember that the BEAST is a distorter of the truth, and when truth is distorted, we often feel this sense of shame. This sense of shame is confronted and challenged most strongly in the light of the day. We often hide our feelings of shame due to our embarrassment and they stay hidden, only to snowball later and bring us further down. You might want to talk about your shameful feelings to your therapist, if not to anyone else. Bring those thoughts and feelings out into the light where you can have a dialogue with them. Most times you will find those shameful things are not even true in the first place, and if they are true somehow, you have a chance to let the strings of shame come untied. They will lose their power in the light of day. When they stay hidden from another, they are insidious. Educate yourself about your illness, do not let your shame stay hidden, as hard as that may be, and eventually you might remember that there is no shame in having a brain illness, just as there is no shame in having a broken bone.

The Fog - I cannot tell you strongly enough about the fatigue of everyday life when you have depression. It's like walking through mud, with your energy zapped, and it is an enormous chore to do the simple everyday chores. My mind is so busy ruminating about the BEAST's agenda that I am tired just from that.

Physically I feel that my body is armored, heavy and lethargic. Activities of daily living are sometimes unbearable. That is why I mentioned earlier that I feel like I'm working on one cylinder. My brain and body are stressed to the max. And my medicines cause some of this lethargy. I do not believe the medical establishment knows why either depression or the medicines given to patients of depression cause lethargy, though they may have some theories. I just know that this feeling of lethargy and demotivation is one of the hardest parts in my recovery. I have found, however, that once I get started despite the difficulty of it, I have a much better day. So, the fog is not much different from anything else when battling the BEAST. We must fight it and move on through the day just as we would if we were not depressed. It is lonely doing this day in and day out, but it is worth the dividends. Venting out your feelings of depression to your therapist helps to a great extent.

The fog can also make you look spaced out. It may appear to others that you are not quite yourself, or that you are just staring at something, but your mind actually is very busy ruminating, with all your focus turned inward. Like I mentioned earlier, a depressed brain is a busy brain in my experience. Sometimes we turn off the outside world because the inside world is so overwhelming. It is at these times that the BEAST is taking control. If you can distract yourself when this starts to happen, you may start to come out of it. However, at other times it just needs to run its course because you may not be in a place where you can distract yourself. Just remind yourself that this, too, shall pass.

Academy Award Worthy - If you have had a depression that has lasted for any length of time, you will know what I mean when I say 'Academy Award Worthy'. Those of us with depression often have to hide their agony by acting normal and keeping their illness underneath the surface. We cannot go around telling people we are in pain because that might push people away. We don't let people see our sick selves so we can have a regular job, a social life, and many other things which people enjoy in a mainstream society. We have to manage the torment deep within ourselves, protect it from the outside world. We must wear a mask at times to function in this world. We have our therapists and our trusted friends, but to function in the way that society wants us to, we have to hide our pain. Some of us are better at it than others. But the irony is that, we are not up for Academy Awards. There is no one to praise you at how well you manage your inside turmoil with your real-world challenges. There are no Oscars. You are a hero, yet no one notices it. It is profoundly lonely in that space.

Chapter Ten: The Side Effects of Medicine, Illness and Knowing the Difference

Is It Medicine or Illness? – I started feeling suicidal on a Monday morning. It was different from my usual suicidal ideation. It was more intense and I fantasized taking all the prescribed pills I had in the house and hopefully be done with it all. I felt I couldn't take it anymore, after years of intense pain and agony. Then I suddenly realized something, I was on a new medicine at a higher dose than I had been. I realized the pills were making me feel this way. But only a few moments earlier I did not have that realization. It all felt like it was coming from me, after all it was my brain that was thinking these thoughts. I called my psychiatrist and conferred with him. He too thought it was the medication causing those extreme thoughts.

This could have been the most disastrous moment of my life for I could have attempted suicide due to the chemical changes in my brain. Thank goodness I had that sudden realization! From this harrowing experience, I can say that we have to be very careful when we are undertaking medicine changes. The medicines are actually messing with our brains, the very organ that creates good thoughts and bad thoughts, good moods and bad moods. And a small white pill nearly pushed me over the edge. I had promised to myself that from that day onwards, I would be much more careful when starting a new medication. I thought that I might even decide to do it in the hospital. I think if I had it there, I would not have had access to a slew of psychotropic medication to swallow in my moments of agony. Also, I would have people around me who might see the difference in my thinking or my personality. It came on so fast, that maybe they would not have seen it either. That got me thinking that it is our responsibility to take precautions when we change medications or adjust them to higher or lower doses. It could be a matter of life or death. I suggest you log how you are feeling when changing medication. Keep a daily log of your moods and thoughts. Let people know if you are feeling worse or more suicidal, especially when having those pills. In my case my hope was vanishing rapidly. I could not see that my situation would get better, my perception had narrowed to the point of hopelessness. Suicide was starting to look like an option, though I was still scared that I would mess it up; precisely the reason why I did not try, and I reached out to my doctor. Not everyone knows the sudden behavior changes after consuming psychotropic medicine, which can be dangerous. So one needs to be extra cautious.

I feel angry, but I am not sure at what or whom. Maybe I am angry with my doctor for not warning me about this. Maybe I am mad at my therapist for not planting this information as a reminder in my head. Maybe I am mad at my illness for taking me to such a dark place to begin with. Maybe I'm angry with all of the above. However, this same medicine taken at a lower dose seems to be helping me, which is good news. When taken in generous doses, it was too soon for my receptor sites to handle. My brain felt awash with no pleasure aka anhedonia, hopelessness and despair. Had I attempted suicide, I would have been labelled as a failure, when I had to undergo heroic attempts to stay alive just 20 hours earlier. I went to work. No one except my sisters and doctor knew what had happened to me. Had I died, no one would have been lauding my long battle with this often-fatal illness and contemplated on how hard and long I had kept myself alive. They would probably have been aggrieved with guilt for not knowing how to help me; they would probably be angry with me for taking my own life. They were unaware that I hadn't had much to do with the choice.

My flash of insight took years of monitoring my illness and being aware of what my process was. I do not think I am any smarter than others who commit suicide due to med changes gone amok, but I am probably more attentive to the changes in my own behavior, and you can be too. So, I leave you with one sentence. Pay attention to any changes in your mood swings or your suicidal thoughts when you change doses or medicines. It could save your life.

Chapter Eleven: Recovery

Recovery is not just about stopping one's symptoms, or getting back to where we were once. Recovering in a nutshell is creating a life for ourselves alongside the BEAST. It is learning new coping skills, finding more support, finding meaning and purpose in one's life. One does not have to settle for stabilization, for one can thrive. We must restructure our lives one day at a time. Recovery will not come to you. Instead, you have to find recovery by going after it, and it's a strenuous exercise. We first have to identify in which aspects of our life we would like to grow, and make an action plan to get there. For example, if I want a better social life, I have to take the risks to get out of my comfort zone and meet new people. If I want a greater intellectual life, I have to find out what interests me and learn more about it. If I want my physical health to be better, I have to learn how to eat right and exercise to the best of my capacity. I cannot dream of doing these things, or put them off for a later date, I must set the goal and just start doing it.

The hardest and most challenging part is getting our brains, our motor, out of park, and into first gear. And, the BEAST will not like you doing this. He will put up a fight. Knowing that the BEAST is a liar will help to put your positive thoughts and actions into perspective and only then you will emerge stronger and healthier. One baby step at a time. And, there is a lot of help out there. Certified Mental Health Peer Specialists can assist you because they "have been there" and they have learned a lot about getting out of the clutches of darkness. They are on the other side even though they still have recovery issues. One can make use of therapy groups, support groups, and one can find a community of individuals with common purpose if one looks hard enough. You are not alone even if it feels like it.

Vulnerability - We must get used to feeling vulnerable if we are to recover. Vulnerability is the feeling of helplessness, imagining or thinking that someone or something can hurt us. Many of us carry around a lot of shame due to the stigma associated with our mental illness. We have internalized it. And the feeling that someone might find out who we really are is scary. We often do not want others to know about our deepest thoughts and feelings stemming from our mental illness, even if we sincerely want to get helped. Usually, people choose a therapist for this, but even the idea of conveying it all to a trained therapist will make us feel vulnerable. However, we must find our courage and talk about those things that scare us or make us feel embarrassed. Otherwise, you will be stuck in your illness.

People cannot read your mind. You have to accept vulnerability as your friend when dealing with a mental illness. The feeling of vulnerability will never be easy, but if you identify the feeling, and understand it, you will have some power over it, and you will not feel so alone. Perhaps, you will also find out that what you are thinking or feeling is very common for those experiencing the same illness. That in itself can bring some relief. If we hold on to our stoicism, we will not get anywhere. If we opt for therapy and not share what is bothering us and wait for the therapist to do all of the work, we are not participating in the therapy; therefore, it cannot help us. To allow yourself to be vulnerable is to eventually find your courage and your bravery. Every human being feels vulnerable at times, but unhealthy means of coping with it interfere with processing it and moving forward. The BEAST might try to mess with you on this, but you are stronger than the BEAST. So, embrace your vulnerability and move on.

Black and White Thinking - We human beings often categorize people, places or things in our mind for the sake of our own convenience. However, they all can be very complex. In order to cope, we often divide them into black or white categories. This shortchanges ourselves and others. If I suffer from constant black or white thinking, I am not giving myself the whole perspective, and just narrowing my vision. If I think "Jane" is either good or bad, then I miss a lot of other aspects about Jane. I have categorized her already, which means I won't be giving myself a chance to get to know her, for I have already decided she is no good. On the other hand, I may come across a liar and think he is all good in the beginning, I could open myself up to danger if I do not notice the intricacies (or the grey areas) of his personality. People are complex and we need to remember that. If someone irritates me a lot, my first instinct is to not like him or her, but with some effort I can come to see his or her perspective, and realize that he/she is not necessarily a bad person, but just a complex person.

Similarly, Black and White Thinking is often the case in many severe mental illnesses because our brains lie to us, and then we react with this type of convenient thinking. It is important that we catch ourselves doing this, for recognizing the complexity of reality is healthy. Also, in this process, we can lessen some of our symptoms.

Perspective Taking - Though it might be difficult and quite challenging a task, it is important that you can stand back and watch yourself have this illness. Watch how the BEAST works and look at it objectively. When our pants are on fire, we can only yell helplessly, but later we can look at the patterns of our illness and be able to tell our doctors how to help us because we can be more informed about our symptoms. We have to become our own spokespersons and advocates so we can best explain what is going on with us and ask for a remedy. For example, I once started noticing that I was getting depressed at 2 pm in the afternoon every day. When I started to question and probe deeper, I started to realize that one of my medicines was wearing off at that time and I was having a rebound effect whereby the depression was not only coming back, but coming back stronger than the original depression.

When we quiz ourselves like a doctor, we begin to see patterns. We can begin to see solutions or theories to fix the problem. Be a detective and ask yourself why things are happening when they do. There may be answers which you never knew existed.

Put yourself in the shoes of your psychiatrist. What information do you think he or she would need to know?

Often, we just tell our symptoms and hope that we can be fixed, but if we think it through more carefully, with more and more details, we can give better information that can lead to a solution. After all, our therapists are only human, which means they are fallible. Not every theory they come up with can be true, or relevant to you. We have to ask ourselves if it resonates with us. If it does not, we need to tell them. A good therapist will be open to the idea that their theory may not be true, and they will not try to force it on you.

It is also important for us to become an active member with our treatment team. Wanting to hear magic words that would "fix" our problems is a nice fantasy, but if you sit around waiting for those rare moments of insight or the right medication, you could be wasting a lot of your time. You have to rely on your 'observing ego', the part of you that watches yourself like an outsider would, analyzing your thoughts and your actions. This may be the most helpful thing you can do for yourself in your recovery.

Soothing Ourselves - Telling myself I will be okay when I am having an episode of panic or depression is an act of falsehood and honestly, it does not soothe me, or make me feel better. If I indulge in it, the BEAST tells me I am lying to myself, which makes me even more miserable. I have found a couple of techniques which do soothe me when I am in some sort of emotional pain. The first one is to use my memory of very loving interactions from my past. Remember what it felt like to be loved unconditionally. Try to remember the warmth of being loved. I can almost hear readers saying "I've never experienced love before" and if so, I want you think about how you receive love. In my own understanding, people who bring me food, love me. Also, people who listen to me without judging me, or have the kindness to just be with me and can understand both my words and my silence, rather than giving advice, love me. That's how I myself experience love. Someone saying "I love you" doesn't work for me. Those are just empty, hollow words for me. My mother saying aloud "I love you", intertwined with verbal abuse during my formative years has been a haunting memory for me, hence those words do not soothe me anymore.

We all have our own ways of feeling and desiring love. Love is manifested in many different ways, but we must realize which ones nurture us the best, so that we can seek out people who can give it, and stay away from those who cannot, especially during a crisis. Additionally, we must become aware of how people love us in ways that may not suit us, but are loving acts all the same. We need to let those count and try to feel it the best way we can.

When you are in intense emotional pain, close your eyes and try to take slow, deep breaths. When you start to calm down a little, try to imagine those recalled memories of being loved. Try to distract from the pain with attention to your breath and your imagery. Keep trying to feel the love that keeps you going even now. Another way to do this is to imagine the people in your life are all there with you, feeling love for you in their hearts. Use your instincts and imagination to hear their words, to feel their love. Let them sit there for as long as you need. Also, you can create your own imagery. Try whatever works best for your mind and soul.

Don't take "I'll be Okay" as the only way to soothe yourself. Be creative, tap into that feeling of love, it will make your eyes moist with tears, but then give you emotional relief. Do not attempt this when you are suffering, but do it when you are well. It will create the much-needed response of relaxation which is good for your brain.

Forgiveness - When suffering with severe brain illness, we often struggle with who to forgive, particularly when we are most symptomatic. Do we forgive the universe, God, or others whose words and/or actions have hurt us? Forgiveness is a gift we give to ourselves to let go of the agony of being hurt by someone or something. Pain that comes and goes intermittently is easier to forgive, but when the pain is chronic and happens daily, or most days, it is an extra burden on us. For some people faith seems to be the solution. That is easy for me when I am feeling well, but when I am struggling beyond my capacity, life does not feel fair. During those trying moments, I am at a loss, trying to figure out whom to forgive. God is my major foe in the act of forgiveness. When the pain will not relent, I cannot comprehend a God that would create this kind of pain for any human. On second thought, maybe God has nothing to do with this, but then I wonder whom else can I blame. You see, the human mind, or at least my mind, tries to make sense of the pain. Yet nothing is sufficient. So, then I blame myself, after all the source of the pain is my brain. Just when I am sure I should blame my brain, that road inevitably leads me back to my creator. So, this business of forgiving has been a hard road for me. This illness for me is so painful and multifaceted that I do not know where to turn sometimes. And, though other people are often wonderfully supportive, I am still alone in my suffering. I feel trapped and angry for this entrapment. Why can't the universe send me a faster form of relief? Yes, speaking of relief, I am grateful for the pills that sometimes ease the pain. I take many of them each day. And, I am grateful for the doctors and therapists out there who try to help me. I want a cure or at least a lengthy reprieve, but that has not happened yet for me, despite doing everything that was recommended, everything I could learn about or think up on my own. At the end of the day, we are fighting with the BEAST. So, what are we to do?

I believe we need to work with our therapists on this issue because it is very complicated and intense. Forgiveness is a gradual process and in attaining it, we must process our feelings of anger, despair, and sometimes lack of fairness. We must, when we can, look at the gifts we have been given and be grateful for them when we feel well. We are not miserable all of the time if we are in recovery. We all have many gifts; we may just have forgotten to focus on them. We also must not forget the gifts that we have received from our suffering, which includes our empathy and concern for others that we derive from this very suffering. In the process, we eventually become better human beings. Our eyes are not without caring for all others who suffer, and for them we can be a soft place to land. It is hard to forgive the circumstances when there is no visible enemy. We only know the pain caused by our mental illness and that it will not go away. So, we have to let go of the blame in the first place, to shift our focus on doing the best we can with what we are given. And, that is not an easy task. We need to not blame ourselves, for we were given a burden; we are not a burden. We are just warriors trying our best to make it through.

We also need to remember that there are reasons for our illness beyond what is humanly possible to understand. We humans are too limited to ever know "why" it has occurred to us. But again, we burden ourselves needlessly when we insist on trying to figure it all out with our limited logic and worldly understanding. So, we need not ask "why" or "why not me" and instead, focus on the goal of recovering as best as we can , while also emphasizing on doing the best that we can in each moment. And, most of all, we must recognize that we are not a failure when we cannot stop the physical and psychological pain.

Maybe one day soon the researchers for brain illnesses will be able to explain the "whys"; until that day comes, we must embark on a journey of forgiveness, empathy and endurance.

Teaching People How To Help You - As adults we all come to a point where we realize people cannot read our minds. Well, most of us do. We all acquire what is called 'maturity'. When you have a major brain illness you not only have to ask for help, but you have to teach people what you need from them. What I need from a therapist is different from what I need from a family member, for they have different gifts to offer. We first need to identify what we need, which takes an enormous effort, and we need to figure out what it is we can expect another human to give us. As we all know, some people are better at giving emotional support than others, and some people are better at cooking a meal for us. We have to discern what each person we want to enlist for help has to give in the first place, or else we could be beating our heads against a wall and feeling worse for begging for help and getting none. I know I have often thought that the people in my life who love me, and know I have a brain illness, would be able to meet my emotional needs at any given time, just like my therapist.

Of course, most of the time they could not, for they are not trained and experienced like a therapist. We have a history of relating to our friends and family members in a different way than a therapist. I do not think I made this assumption out of nothing. So, we can get very aggravated if we expect people to shrink our brains for us when they have no training. Most people have something to offer us, but we have to first figure out what it is. For example, my two sisters are great at doing things for me. They came over to my house and cleaned out my closet. However, had I needed some feedback on how I was feeling, these two wonderful women would not be my first choice to go to for that. Reading my mind and interpreting my behavior is not their forte. But, some of my friends who also suffer from a severe mental illness are great at emotional feedback, and so it is smart to ask them for this kind of help. Everyone has their strengths and their limitations and we need to honor those. It increases our chances that our needs get met. In this world, we are blessed to have people with whom we laugh and those with whom we cry. Sometimes we get lucky and find someone who can do both. You can always find someone with whom to bare your soul if you look closely enough around you. It will save you both time and trouble as you do not need to get emotionally shut down by someone who you know is not adept at feelings.

Asking for help should be as direct as possible without being aggressive or overtly needy. Starting with "I" statements is a good start, as in "I need you to just listen to what I am about to say, but really am not looking for you to fix me, please just hear." Do not be too disappointed if the person cannot comply with your request; but just use the responses of him/her as a learning experience. People come with a variety of offerings. If you look for a need to be met by a person who cannot give it to you, you are going to feed the BEAST. The BEAST will whisper to you silently: "I told you no one could help you; you are alone." I say this, but yet, I often do this very thing. However, as I age, I am getting better at checking out my needs and my options with people. Once again, we need a team! And what better time to start than now.

It is also a good lesson to let people help you. We live in a society that teaches us that helping others is what matters. However, there are two sides to this coin. When you are the one who is in need of help, someone has to be the "helpee", and that is how it works. Perhaps one of the existential lessons of this illness is learning to let people help us, to open our doors for that person. This is worth pondering.

Community - Fighting the BEAST by ourselves is a task we cannot ever accomplish. We need community to combat it powerfully. We need a place where we can be heard and also hear others while bonding with them. It can be helpful to our self- esteem, and helpful to us too, when we are involved in a community with like-minded people. Community comes with a commitment to be a part of a group, where you have the opportunity to get outside of our own mind. The bond within community members enhances structure, meaning, and responsibility in our lives. As I mentioned earlier, the mental health Clubhouses that are around the country and the world provide structure and also a strong sense of community.

It is especially nice to have friends with a mental illness because they understand the struggle of dealing daily with symptoms of a mental illness. Your churches and synagogues are a good place to find a supportive, empathetic community. Also, support groups are a good place to look for. There are book clubs and other social supports out there if you just look for what you are interested in. The more support you can find within a community, the better it will serves your mental health. It beats the hell out of ruminating.

Conclusion

These ideas on how to battle the BEAST have been shared from my own experience, and from knowing and talking with many others who also suffer from severe depression, schizoaffective disorder, and bipolar disorder. I hope the ideas presented in the book, coupled with my own journey have been helpful in some way, and I hope that in your darkest hours you can recall some of these coping mechanisms to get you through the horrible times of suffering. Though I have reiterated throughout the book that you are not alone in your suffering, in those dark moments, it can sure feel like it. Remember that the BEAST is a formidable opponent; the more you know about your own BEAST, the more you can figure out how to get untangled from him.

As I conclude my final thoughts, I feel honored to share some of my own insights, having come to terms with my illness that I openly discuss with you in this book. It was a long, arduous journey of reflection and introspection. If one person can gain strength and understanding of his/her illness, then it will be worth every tear I shed along the way.

What strikes me emotionally as I was editing the book is the deep degree of fortitude I have developed over the years of my illness and how it seemingly kept me alive through various phases of my crisis. Where did it come from, I often queried? I must have inherited fortitude from both my parents as I witnessed it in them in different degrees while growing up. Ironically though, I think I inherited this trait more from my mother. The mother whom I didn't quite understand most of my life, the mother that I did not get along with until she was old and ill. However, all that being said and done, she was the mother who deep down loved and only wanted the best for her three children.

As my parting words, I would only say: embrace your inner fortitude. It may just save your life like it did mine.

Bibliography

A Guide to Mental Health for Families and Careers of People with Intellectual Disabilities: Holt, Gershine, Gratsa, Anastasia and Bouras, Nick, (London and Philadelphia, Jessica Kingsley, 2004).

A Mood Apart: 1998. By Peter C. Whybrow. Harper Paperbacks, 384 pages.

Another Kind of Madness: A Journey Through the Stigma and Hope of Mental Illness: Hinshaw, Stephen P. (New York, St. Martin's Press, 2017)

An Unquiet Mind: A Memoir of Moods and Madness: Jamison, Kay Redfield (New York: Vintage Books, 2011). Translated into 30 languages. On the New York Times Bestseller List for five months).

Bipolar Disorder: A Guide for patients and Families, 2nd edition, 2006. By Francis Mark Mondimore. The Johns Hopkins University Press, 304 pages.

Call Me Anna: The Autobiography of Patty Duke: Duke, Patty and Turan, Kenneth (Toronto; New York, Bantam Book, 1987).

Cognitive Behavioral Therapy: Albin, Jayme and Bailey, Eileen (New York: Penguin Group, 2014).

Coping with Stress: Improve Your Mental Health and Find Peace in Your Everyday Life, Sockolov, Matthew (A complete guide to wellness, 2021). () Great Cover – See Amazon.

Crime, Punishment and Mental Illness: Law and the Behavioral Sciences in Conflict: Erickson, Patricia E. and Erickson, Steven K., (New Brunswick, NJ, Rutgers University Press, 2088).

Delusional Disorder: Paranoia and Related Illnesses: Munro, Alistair, (Cambridge and New York: Cambridge University Press, 1999).

Going to Extremes: Mood Disorders and Schizophrenia: Myers, David, and Jamison, Kay Redfield (San Francisco; Kanopy Streaming, 2014, 2016).

I Am Not Sick, I Don't Need Help! How to Help Someone to Accept Treatment: 2020, by Xavier Amadore (20th Anniversary Edition) New York, Vida Press.

I'm Telling The Truth, But I'm Lying: Essays, Ikpi, Bassey., (New York; Harper Perennial, 2019)

Kübler-Ross, E. (1970). On death and dying. Collier Books/Macmillan Publishing Company.

Living Without Depression and Manic Depression: A Workbook for Maintaining Mood Stability. 1994 by Mary Ellen Copeland, New Harbinger Publications, 263 pages.

Loving Someone with Bipolar Disorder: 2004, by Julie A. Fast and John D. Preston. New Harbinger Publications, 208 pages.

Manic-Depressive Illness: Recurrent Depression and Bipolar Disorders: Goodwin, Frederick K. and Jamison, Kay Redfield (New

York: Oxford University Press, 2007). Comprehensive. Written for mental health professionals. The classic textbook on bipolar disorder.

Media Madness: Public Images of Mental Illness: Wahl, Otto F. (New Brunswick, NJ, Rutgers Press, 1995).

Modern Madness: An Owner's Manual: Cheney, Terri (Hachette Books, New York, 2020)

My Lovely Wife in the Psych Ward: A Memoir: Lukach, Mark (New York: Harper Wave, 2017)

Nothing to Hide: Mental Illness in the Family: Beard, Jean J. and Gillespie, Peggy: (New York: New Press: Distributed by W.W. Norton and Co., 2002)

Out of the Cave: Stepping into the Light when Depression Darkens What You See: Hodges, Chris (Nashville TN: Thomas Nelson, 2021)

Taking Charge of Bipolar Disorder: A 4-Step Plan for you and Your Loved Ones to Manage the Illness and Create Lasting Stability. 2006. By Julie A. Fast and John Preston. Waner Wellness, 320 pages.

The Bipolar Disorder Survival Guide, Third Edition:

What You and Your Family Need to Know: Miklowitz, David J., (New York; Guildford Press, 2019)

Touched with Fire: Manic-Depressive Illness and the Artistic Temperament: Jamison, Kay Redfield (New York: Free Press Paperbacks, 1994).

Understanding Mental Disorders: Your Guide to DSM-5 ® (Washington, DC: American Psychiatric Association, 2015)

Websites

bpHOPE.com – An online periodical focusing on Bipolar Disorder.

Free online periodical: Weekly information and inspiration.

Offers quarterly magazines both online and print formats.

Choosingtherapy.com – The 17 best books about bipolar disorder as of August 20, 2021.

Clubhouseintl.org - Clubhouse International find a clubhouse in your area- or if there's not one, get one started with other interested adults

Mayoclinic.org

Mentalhealth.net – Their selections for good bipolar disorder books.

National Alliance on Mental Illness - nami.org National Institute of Health - nih.gov

National Institute of Mental Health - nimh.nih.gov

Simpleandpractical.com – Books for patients and families with bipolar disorder.

Webmd.com

World Health Organization - who.int

Periodicals

The Week's Top Mental Health News: Includes US and International News as well as Texas News: Hogg Foundation for Mental

Health/The University of Texas at Austin/Division of Diversity and Community Engagement: Free Online at https://hogg.utexas.

Acknowledgments

I would like to thank Jim Davis, author and my friend, for all his time and expertise that led to this book being published. I would like to thank Ruth Josenhans, LPC, and The Director of PLAN (People Living Active Now) Mental Health Clubhouse in Dallas, Texas for her steadfast belief in me and her tireless efforts to continually make PLAN a safe and nurturing environment. PLAN is a program of Jewish Family Service of Greater Dallas. I would also like to thank my dear friend, Tracy Schanbacher, for her constant encouragement and Lopa Banerjee for her proficiency in editing. In addition, I would like to mention my sister, Bonnie Cohen Levy, who helped get this book finished by formatting and typing the manuscript and lovingly pestering me to finish in ways where I was procrastinating. My gratefulness goes to Dr. Howard Smith, my psychiatrist of many years, who tirelessly worked with me to find the right med combination for my condition. I truly would like to thank my therapist, Kathy Reilly, for always telling me "Call me if you need me!" which I believe saved my life. Lastly, an abundance of gratitude to all of those affected by mental illness and their families for teaching me much of what I know today.

About the Author

Pamela G. Cohen, M.A. has been a mental health consumer for over 41 long years overcoming many struggles which derailed and devastated her life when she was only 19 years old. As a client, she still seeks the advice from various therapists, psychologists and psychiatrists to help manage her clinical depression, mania and mixed episodes i.e., bipolar disorder.

From the other side of the couch, Pamela is quite accomplished despite the intense mental health challenges she continues to endure. Over her lifetime she earned her Master's Degree in clinical psychology, became a massage therapist, a professional tennis instructor, a bereavement counselor and a Director of Education/Socialization for people with serious and persistent mental illness (SMI). Pamela never thought she could achieve any of these goals, but she did, and her wish is that others will reach their goals too.

Pamela presently works as a Mental Health Peer Specialist in the Dallas, TX area and uses her lived experience to assist others who have SMI.

Made in the USA
Monee, IL
27 June 2023

37796840R00090